EASY
TAO

EASY TAO

BY SIMON CHANG
AND FRITZ POKORNY

Photographs by Larry Williams
Cover Design by Robbin Henderson
© 1988 by China Books

ISBN 0-8351-1833-9

Printed in the United States of America by

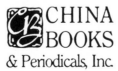

CHINA
BOOKS
& Periodicals, Inc.

Original Austrian edition by Lechner-Verlag, 1987

Contents

Preparatory Exercises

Twelve Main Exercises

About This Book

This book contains a description of a set of traditional Chinese exercises designed to strengthen the body, heighten vitality and the overall energy, while at the same time inducing new spiritual and physical strength.

Easy Tao* is a comprehensive, coherent system of exercises based on thousands of years of experience, the principles of Chinese medicine, the science of Qi (also written as Ch'i), and the vital force inherent in the human body.

In Chinese medicine one central aspect has always been to improve the balance of this vital Qi by means of physical exercises of all kinds. Such exercises were designed to either prevent loss of vital Qi or repair an imbalance that had already occurred.

The system of Easy Tao, as we call it, is a traditional and ancient teaching that was previously accessible only to members of the Chinese imperial families. Its original name was Wai Tan Gong, which means "Exercise of External Cinnabar." This Tan (Cinnabar) is a central concept of Chinese medico-alchemical systems. In these exercises of "inner alchemy," physical exercise as well as the technics of meditation and concentration were used to enhance the inner powers in order to raise one's physical energy and reach higher states of consciousness.

Just as for its European counterpart, Chinese alchemy has always put great emphasis on the element mercury as a symbol of the flexible and changing

* The term "Tao" comes from Taoism, one of the main philosophical systems of China. The two terms are also written "Dao" and "Daoism" in the pinyin method of Romanization.

nature of the human mind. Symbolisms of this sort may not appeal much to our modern minds, trained in logical reasoning and scientific thought, but we must not forget that these systems evolved from patient and detailed observation of nature. So even if their terminology may sound a little too imprecise and vague for our ears, we must still acknowledge that these systems can be applied today with good results. And we may even be surprised at how precisely concepts and ideas from another culture of some 2,000 years ago can still be put to use today.

Complete medical systems like those of the Chinese are few in number. The Egyptians, in fact, had medical theories that somewhat resembled those of the Chinese. But what makes the Chinese system unique is the unbroken chain of tradition that has continued for over 2,000 years.

The earliest reference to concepts and terms related to Chinese traditional medicine, as it is now known, date back to the second millennium B.C., while the oldest known treatise on Chinese medicine dates to the 3rd century B.C. This work gives a systematic synopsis of the basic concepts of Chinese medicine in some detail.

A continuity like this is unparalleled not only in medical science, which in the West evolved to its present state within the last 600 years or so, but also in every other aspect of culture.

With a tradition this ancient, it is not surprising to find that Chinese medicine surpasses its Western counterpart in many aspects.

Whereas western science in general has always sought to divide its object into ever smaller components and details, and has thereby piled up an

incredible amount of knowledge in a sometimes rather pedantic manner, it has often lost sight of the whole that makes up these components. Chinese medicine has always looked at the human body as a whole and has always tried to grasp the totality that keeps this body alive. Even though this approach may seem somewhat vague, we must admit that the results have provided the Chinese with knowledge and techniques that have to be acknowledged by western science. Western doctors are, of course, at loss as how to account for the efficiency of these techniques, of which acupuncture is probably the most accepted these days.

This book is not an iconoclastic attempt to do away with western medicine and deny its benefits, but we do hope that the reader will be able to lay aside these ideas for a time and learn about the theoretical and practical aspects of Easy Tao.

In Search of Lost Harmony

Easy Tao has been known since the times of the Tang Dynasty as a set of exercises to complement martial arts techniques. It is a traditional technique to awaken and strengthen the Qi, the vital force of the human body. In later times, Easy Tao was handed down exclusively within the imperial family. It resurfaced again only in this century when it was rediscovered and remodeled with the help of ancient texts. Starting in Taiwan, where over a 100,000 people are now practising Easy Tao, it has spread through southeast Asia, mostly through countries with large Chinese populations. Now Easy Tao has reached the United States and it is spreading rapidly.

What do you have to know about Easy Tao?

Easy Tao works through simple movements of the body that can be done even by old and sick people. These movements stimulate the flow of the vital force that is the source of all other energies in the human body. If the vital force can flow through the body without encountering resistance or blockage, all functions of the body will be strengthened, the mind will work effortlessly, and the body will be regenerated and toned.

Easy Tao is also called the "Hundred Days Exercise," because it only takes a hundred days of constant patient practice to receive the first obvious results.

How do you know you're doing it right?

The muscles and tendons of the body are strengthened and elasticized almost imperceptibly, the breath and the heartbeat become more regular, blood and Qi are cleaned and strengthened, the meridians and the nervous system are made more resistant, and the overall condition of the body improves along with mental energy—in other words, a relaxing balance of all physical and mental functions is achieved. We must be aware of the fact that Easy Tao is not just another kind of gymnastics and that it also has no connection with yoga or other physical exercises. Easy Tao is a unique system benefiting both body and mind by stimulating the vital forces of Qi and thereby making it more resistant to illness and stress.

You need to do the exercises in just a little space, perhaps about the size of a bed. And you need to do them for a little time each day. Thus, even in the most limited and pressing circumstances, you will be able to practice. Easy Tao is an ideal way for staying fit and keeping in shape, with a minimum of effort.

Every person's body responds when they start to practice Easy Tao. But depending on individual fitness and physical shape, these reactions will manifest themselves in different ways at different times. For someone who is well trained and in good physical shape, there will seem to be no obvious response at first, whereas for someone who suffers from illness or who is recovering from an illness the exercises can produce slight pain, exhaustion, dizziness and other symptoms in the beginning. All these are no cause for alarm. They just show that the body is getting used to the new exercise. These symptoms actually prove that something positive is happening in your body and that Easy Tao is exerting a healing influence. If the symptoms become too painful, one should pause a little bit before continuing the exercise.

The force that Easy Tao aims to activate is Qi, a flow of energy in the body. If the Qi starts to flow without restraint, this will after a while produce a slight trembling or shaking of the corresponding part of the body. One therefore has to be prepared to encounter this phenomenon when exercising and not be alarmed by it. The trembling is a sign that healthy Qi is flowing through the body in a continuous stream, and that the exercises are being done correctly. If you find the shaking uncomfortable, you can always stop it by contracting the muscles of the corresponding part of the body.

To arouse the optimal flow of Qi in your body, stay completely relaxed and calm, without nervousness or impatience. While doing the exercises the trembling of Qi can also be accompanied by a feeling of numbness in the affected parts of the body, spreading from the ends of the fingers and toes towards the trunk of the body. When the vibrations cease, it is a sign that body and mind are relaxed and filled with vital Qi. You will see that your legs or arms feel warm and loose. Easy Tao not only benefits one's own body and mind, but in China the powers aroused by Easy Tao are also used to heal and strengthen other people.

Easy Tao is a simple but nonetheless efficient system of twenty exercises. The first set described in this book are called "preparatory practice." They warm up and prepare the body for the main exercises.

The main ones are exercises nine to twenty. Older people or people who are recovering from an illness should first practise only the preparatory exercises and move on to the main ones after they have the feeling that they have mastered the first set. One should always keep in mind that the goal of the exercises is not to get exhausted or out of breath. So at the beginning take things easy. Patience, determination, perseverance, and relaxation are the most important elements for success with Easy Tao. In short, you need to pay attention to these things when exercising:

RELAXATION. The body must remain completely relaxed when doing the exercises. Tension in any part of the body will slow down the beneficial results.

INNER CALMNESS. It is important to concentrate on the exercise with calmness and inner joy. Do not force yourself to do anything, but try to keep your mind as free of thoughts as possible. Just watch your thoughts calmly as they arise and float through your mind.

CORRECT POSTURE. Try to always keep your body in the correct posture as described. The main points are: The upper part of the body must remain upright, but not overly straight. The back must also remain straight, but should not be stretched stiffly. The small of your back should be pulled forward slightly. The tongue should touch the top of the palate; it closes the circuit of energy along the axis of your body.

The best time for practice is in the morning or in the evening. But you can also practice during a break from work. Just bear in mind that you should never practice with a full stomach.

When you first begin practicing you can do the exercise for shorter amounts of time and then slowly increase the duration of exercise as you get acquainted with the motions. The ideal duration for the exercise should be between 20 and 25 minutes daily.

Yin and Yang

What is the secret that lies behind the calmness and serenity of the Chinese way of life? It is Chinese philosophy, a thought system based on age-old observations of nature, a basic attitude towards life and towards all natural phenomena. In this philosophical system everything has its place and all things are subject to a basic principle of order. Let us try to understand the main elements of this system and get acquainted with its most prominent concepts and ideas.

ORDER OF THE UNIVERSE

According to Chinese belief, all of the universe is permeated by one basic principle of function that manifests itself in every part of the universe, no matter how big or how small. This all-embracing principle governing every process in the universe is called "Tao."

The word Tao originally meant something like "road" or "street," but in later times it also came to designate a concept close to the Greek idea of "cosmos"—order, harmony, the organized whole. This is why this word was also eventually used for the universe, creation in constant harmony, and following strict laws and rules. Tao can also be used for the law, the basic principle, and the entity that covers the whole universe and is standing behind all phenomena and their origin and disappearance.

Nature works according to the law of the Tao. The courses of the stars, the change of the seasons, the growth of plants and animals, birth and death, the circle of life - behind all these phenomena lies the force of the Tao, which maintains the harmony of all processes in the universe.

MAN AND THE UNIVERSE

What is the position of man in this system of natural philosophy? Man's consciousness and his awareness of himself and of the world create a certain contradiction to the Tao. This is because man is always tempted to believe that he can change the course of things and force his will upon nature. This may go well for some time, but in the long run it always turns out that the laws of nature prevail. All that man achieves, in his attempts to alter nature, is to cause harm and disharmony in nature—and in himself. He will not live in harmony with the circle of nature, but instead chooses to oppose the elementary laws of life.

At first this will just cause a constant drain on man's energy reserves and eventually ruins his health. The original, natural balance is lost only to be replaced by a tense and frustrated state of being. Instead of always renewing and recharging one's own physical powers by living in harmony with Tao/nature, man wastes all his energy working against what actually are his most important needs. Instead of always deepening and renewing his harmony with the Tao, he gets further and further away from the state of harmony. All his inner energy is burnt up in exhausting rituals of civilization.

The idea of Easy Tao is not, of course, to tell people to drop out and withdraw from "the world." One need not enter a mountain recluse and become a hermit. Nobody has to renounce the world. The only thing to pay attention to is the fact that one should adapt to the law of constant change and counterbalance in nature.

One should not to do anything excessively, but try to find a rhythm of tension and relaxation, calmness and activity, just as day follows night and winter follows summer in nature.

HUMAN NATURE

What is the reason that Chinese thought and philosophy, in its quest for principles of existence, has always oriented itself to nature? The answer can be found in the fact that Chinese society has always been agricultural, for an unbroken period of several thousand years. The necessities of agriculture led to exact, patient observation of nature. The Chinese studied the constant process of change in nature and described its laws. So for the Chinese it was obvious that human life must not be looked upon as separated from the change of seasons, the laws of nature. And the Chinese looked for the basic principles that could explain the variety of phenomena of nature, as well as of human life itself. This underlying principle was found in Tao, the highest goal of human thought and action, the cause of all forms of life. Tao is not only a philosophical, theoretical way, but also a practical sense for everyday life. The unity and harmony of the Tao is one of the most fundamental and profound teachings of Tao philosophy. The attainment of this goal is in no way connected to ideas of evolution or progress, which prevail in western philosophy.

Actually, in the strict sense of the word, the concept of progress does not even exist in Chinese philosophy. Attaining harmony with the Tao is in fact nothing but turning back to one's own roots, to the deepest and most original principle of existence. In this is a fundamental contradiction to the thoughts of evolution and eschatology upheld by western culture, which is based on a Judaeo-Christian philosophy that promises perfect life only in the distant future.

In Chinese concepts of life, unity with the basic principle of the universe means nothing but the insight that life is a continuous flow of change, which man cannot escape. Calmness, harmony, vitality, and joy can be attained by man only if he gives into this natural rhythm of life. Flexibility and adaptability are the highest ideals in life. One oft cited metaphor is the quality of water. Water is humble and naturally always moves to the lowest place it can find. Water flows around every obstacle it encounters in its course and can still, just by the force of its continuous flow, erode even the hardest rocks. Flexibility and steadiness—these are the two main virtues of Tao. By applying these two principles one can save one's strength and still reach one's goals.

THE VIRTUOUS RULER

Harmony with the laws of nature also constitutes the main element of Chinese theories of government. The ruler of a country need only act in accordance with the unchangeable laws of nature. He thus rules his country in such a way that it is almost unnecessary for him to take any active measures of government. This is the teaching of "not-doing," Wu Wei. According to this theory, man must not try to influence the natural course of events, much less even try to induce abrupt change.

The task of a Virtuous Ruler lies in discovering disharmony and imbalance and in trying to re-establish the natural state of harmony when such imbalance is detected. If this principle is applied to as large an organism as the state and to the order of the complete universe, then by analogy it must also be applied on a small scale to the human body. And because all things happen in harmony with the Tao, there must be a parallelism between microcosm and macrocosm. By leading a harmonious life in accordance with the Tao, it is thus possible to stabilize the harmony of one's family or one's country and make a small-scale contribution to the functioning and harmony of society. This is the working of the Tao that interconnects all systems in the universe.

UNITY AND DIVERSITY

How can this unifying principle of creation bring about the actual diversity of the world? Chinese cosmology explains this process by the continuous changes between opposites that can be observed in nature. These opposites constitute the most characteristic quality of nature. Phenomena like day and night or heat and cold signify the existence of a dynamic, dualistic principle, the archetypal pair of opposites Yin and Yang. These two opposites spring forth from the formless, immutable Tao. They generate the variety and diversity of nature by constantly mixing and mutually influencing each other in more and more complex constellations.

Tao is the principle of existence. Yin and Yang are dynamic principles inseparable from Tao that bring the element of motion, change and variety into the play of cosmic powers. The concepts of Yin and Yang have been known in Chinese for a long time. Originally Yin meant the northern slope of a mountain and Yang meant the southern slope. The meaning of Yin eventually came to be extended to that which is shadowy, dark, quiet, and female. And the southern, sunny side came to designate the light, warm, active male principle. These two principles can be discerned in every single thing in the world. The forces of Yin and Yang are the basic, driving powers of life. Nothing can exist without either of these two principles, and also everything can be classified either as Yin or Yang according to its main qualities. At the same time neither of these two principles is more valuable than the other; neither is superior or inferior to the other. One cannot be thought of without the other. Wherever there is Yin, there also exists, at least latently, a corresponding Yang, and vice versa. If one knows this simple basic law, it is easy to predict which Yang must inevitably follow a certain Yin. The slightest imbalance on one side will without doubt bring about a reaction from the other side, and thereby neutralize this imbalance. In the following table you can find a few pairs of characteristic opposites very common in Chinese accounts:

YIN	YANG
Night	Day
Cloudy	Sunny
Fall	Spring
Winter	Summer
West	East
North	South
Below	Above
Inside	Outside
Cold	Hot
Water	Fire
Dark	Bright
Moon	Sun
Female	Male

Yin and Yang and the Human Body

The organs of the human body, too, are classified into one of the two Yin and Yang categories. So are the different types of energy and channels of energy of the human body, which we shall discuss in detail at a later point. For first reference we give the following diagram:

YIN	YANG
Liver	Gall Bladder
Heart	Small Intestine
Spleen	Stomach
Lungs	Large Intestine
Kidney	Bladder
Pericardium	Three Body Cavities

Being healthy, in Chinese medical theory, means that the forces of Yin and Yang in the body are in a well-balanced state. Whenever this balance is disturbed, illness and discomfort result. Since Chinese medicine sees illness coming from an imbalance of powers within the body, the main aim of medical therapy is to keep up or restore the balance between Yin and Yang forces of the organism.

It must be made clear at this point that Yin and Yang are not two absolute qualities that exist separately from each other, but they should be thought of as always being in relation to one another. Within one large unit that is either Yin or Yang, you can further discern opposites of Yin and Yang that thereby represent a Yin within a Yang or a Yang within a Yin. For instance, surfaces can be classified as Yang and the insides as Yin. Therefore the surface of a Yang organ is Yang, whereas the inside of the organ is Yin seen in relation to its surface. In this way a pair of opposites can be observed down to the smallest articles or components, down to the very nucleus of the atom.

The regulation of the supply of energy in a body is controlled by the balance of relatively cool Yin energies and hot Yang energies. These regulate the life functions and distribute energy from food and respiration evenly to all organs of the body.

Easy Tao is a well-balanced system of exercises based upon these insights. The exercises stimulate the smooth flow and exchange of these energies within the body. The organs of the body are toned and the overall health improves, because Easy Tao helps to repair misfunctions in the balance of energies in the body. If the exercises are continued for a long time, they will also raise body and mind to a higher level of energy. The body will be more resistant to illness and the mind will be able to function with better concentration and work effortlessly.

Do not be deceived by the seeming simplicity of the exercises. They are based on a well-proven system of natural harmony between all things in nature. Easy Tao cannot be compared to any system of gymnastics or similar exercises in the western tradition of physical culture. Easy Tao directly addresses the subtle system of energy exchange in the human body. Chinese medicine has known and applied the workings of this system to the treatment of physical and mental disorders of all sorts for thousands of years with great success.

The secret behind Easy Tao is the achievement of a balanced state of Yin and Yang energies within the body. Whoever practices Easy Tao can tune his body and mind to the basic law of nature, the principle of Tao.

The Five Elements

Next to the basic principle of the Tao and the dynamic pair of antagonists Yin and Yang, there is another set of concepts that plays an important role in Chinese Philosophy and medical theory. These are the five elements that are crucial to the explanation of certain laws and processes and interdependencies in nature. Not unlike the four elements of ancient Greek philosophy—Earth, Water, Fire and Air—which were an important part of European philosophy up to the end of the Middle Ages, the Chinese attributed a set of archetypal qualities to matter that helped them to classify natural phenomena. The Chinese elements are called Wood, Fire, Earth, Metal and Water. The element Wood in the Greek tradition can be equated to the Chinese element Metal, only the element Wood does not have a counterpart in the European system.

This system of five elements was incorporated in a wide variety of Chinese classifications of nature. The system was used to prove the interdependence of all aspects of nature and the universal validity of this classification of five elements. Even emotions and sensations were taken into this complex system.

There are two chains of mutual relation that can be observed among the five elements. One of them is the relation of mutual origin and the other one that of mutual destruction.

Wood brings forth Fire; Fire produces ashes (Earth); Earth yields Metal, which can be transformed into a liquefied state of aggregation (Water). Water, in turn, nourishes plants and thereby produces Wood. The system of mutual destruction can be observed with Wood destroying Earth, Earth destroying Water, Water extinguishing Fire, Fire destroy-ing Metal, and Metal cutting Wood.

We have put together a little table showing a few of the concepts classified under the categories of the five elements:

WOOD	FIRE	EARTH	METAL	WATER
Spring	Summer	intercalary month	Autumn	Winter
sour	bitter	sweet	spicy	salty
blue	red	yellow	white	black
wind	heat	humidity	dryness	cold
eyes	tongue	mouth	nose	ears
east	south	center	west	north
liver	heart	spleen	lungs	kidneys
gall bladder	small intestine	stomach	large intestine	bladder

In accordance with the law of correspondence between microcosm and macrocosm, the theory of the five elements is also applied in Chinese medicine. Thus we find this corresponding classification of mutual interdependence and attribution for the organs of the body:

	YIN-ORGANS	YANG-ORGANS
Wood	Liver	Gall Bladder
Fire	Heart	Small Intestine
Earth	Spleen	Stomach
Metal	Lungs	Large Intestine
Fire	Pericardium	Three Body Cavities

The relation of mutual destruction and mutual origin, which we know from the five elements, find their counterpart in a relation of mutual stimulation and sedation in the organs of the body. If, for instance, through acupuncture or other therapeutical techniques or medication the Fire-organ heart is being stimulated, there will be a corresponding stimulation and sedation in other parts of the body in relation to the five elements. When the Earth-organ spleen is stimulated, the Metal-organ lung will be sedated. Likewise if the Earth-organ stomach is being sedated, this will result in subsequent sedation of the function of the small intestine and in stimulation of the bladder. This is, of course, just a schematic rendering of the principle of the five elements in Chinese medical theory, and there can also be found a number of other relations between the organs of the body that are much more complex and intricate. The basic principle of mutual relation, however, always remains the same. This principle can be applied by using an approach of indirect therapy, whereby it is possible to abstain from directly influenc-ing the function of an afflicted organ and perhaps further impairing the harmonious household of energy of the body and causing further chain reactions of affliction.

This is a very wise and ingenious way of medical therapy that has for a very long time been completely disregarded by western doctors, who often choose to apply therapy according to the most obvious symptoms of a disease, overlooking the fact that due to the complicated working of this system of interdependence the cause for illness might very well be found in a part of the body seemingly unaffected by the symptoms.

Even though the Chinese theory might at first sound unscientific and abstruse, this system of the five elements, like the rest of Chinese medical science is based on close and thoughtful observation of nature. It can be very useful to modern doctors if they choose to accept it. Actually, in judging the merits of any kind of theory, the most important factor should always be its practical applicability. There is no reason to close one's eyes to useful, helpful things only because the terminology employed seems to be "unscientific" and because our science at present is not able to explain them.

Easy Tao is a set of exercises that has its origins in this system of medical theory. It makes use of the mutual relations of organs and of the elements under which they are classified. So every single exercise not only benefits one special organ for which it may be designed, it also benefits the other organs that are connected to it in this system of mutual interdependence of the five elements.

The Qi

Let us now take a look at the mysterious forces that connect the organs of the body, and which transport energy according to the laws of mutual interdependence. The key to the working of this system is the concept of Qi, the force of life and the energy maintaining and supporting life. Whereas western natural science has always tried to enter deeper and deeper into the details of things, dissecting and analyzing them, it has often lost sight of the whole. Generally western natural science has put questions about the fundamental force of life into the realm of philosophy or religion. In Chinese medical science, one of the main objects of study has always been to discover the mechanisms of the basic force of life itself so as to have the key to all other phenomena. And while the theoretical renderings of these observations may sound somewhat obscure, even western medicine must by now admit that in practice one can work with the concepts that this quest for the basic force of life has discovered.

The concept that we are talking about is Qi. The word originally meant "air." For Chinese in ancient times air was just empty space with nothing visible in it. They thus came to believe that this "air" must be some kind of energy that man takes in with each breath. We know similar concepts from other cultures, such as "ether" in the European tradition, or the word "prana" from India, which originally meant breath or air and later also came to have the meaning of energy. The foundation behind these concepts is the idea that some force of life enters the body through breathing and circulates inside the body in certain channels.

This energy of Qi can be divided into several subgroups. First of all it is the life force of every living being, human or animal. There is no life without the Qi. The Qi regulates all processes of life. When the Qi leaves the body, death results immediately. Qi is present in every living being from the moment of conception; it is formed through the energies of semen and ovulum. Qi, through its continuous function, generates the condition for the energy that enters the body through nourishment and breathing to be transformed and absorbed. This form of Qi the Chinese call the Qi of the Former Heaven. It is the basic energy of the body, and it is the kind of energy that will be awakened in the body through Easy Tao. This Qi is sent vibrating through the energy channels of the body. It must constantly be supplemented by Qi from food and respiration, which is the second type of Qi, called the Qi of the Latter Heaven. This second type of Qi enters the body through the lungs and is channeled into the energy circulation system originating there. There are altogether twelve such channels of energy, each corresponding to one of the organs shown in the last diagram. Along these channels, or meridians as they are called, there are certain points that have to be stimulated if one wishes to treat the organ of the body corresponding to this meridian. If the Qi can flow along these meridians freely without encountering any blockage, this means that the energy household of the body is completely balanced and that the body is healthy.

The Qi that is extracted from food will also be channeled into this circle of energy. The stomach absorbs it and from there it is channeled directly into the lung meridian. Thus, Qi circulates inside the body from two different sources in one system and benefits the body in two different forms:

First, as nourishing Qi, which has cooler, slower and more subtle qualities and travels along the meridians and the blood vessels. This Qi moves mainly on the inside of the body and is classified as Yin.

Second, as protecting Qi, having a hot, fast and aggressive nature that warms the surface of the body and mobilizes the protective forces of the body. This Qi is classified as Yang.

The flow of Qi regulates the metabolism and balance of the body fluids. If the flow of Qi is slowed down or interrupted, discomfort and illness will result.

The flow of Qi can also be interrupted or slowed down for therapeutical purposes, for instance slowed down to stop overproduction by a certain organ or to stimulate or slow down the function of another organ connected with it through the system of mutual interdependence of the five elements.

Another important form of bodily energy is seen in the sexual Qi, produced in the shape of sperm and ovulum. Because this Qi has the potential to create new life, there is an extraordinary concentration of it in the reproductive cells, and their strong energy content makes them extremely important to the body. There is a long tradition of techniques for preserving the energy of the reproductive cells and for recycling it into the bodily system of energy. This is one way the ancient Chinese sought to raise the vitality of the body and also to train and refine the mind.

Sperm energy, or "essence" as it is called, plays an important role in Chinese medical theory.

Another important element of the energy system in the body are the body fluids, which can be discerned into Yin and Yang fluids. Yang fluid is hot and quick in nature. It is the basis for body secretions such as sweat and urine. The Yin fluid is cool and slow and mainly serves to elastify joints and tendons and keep the locomotor system "lubricated."

Still another principle in Chinese medicine is the concept of mind, which is not a metaphysical principle but the carrier of the mental functions. Mind, like Qi, arises from the union of reproductive cells and thereby is not a supernatural force but the energy that enables man to have perception. It is the seeing of the eyes, or the hearing of the ears. Mind also depends on the harmony of all physical functions and on the balance of Qi within the bodily energy system. If the mind is weakened, this can bring about impairment of the sense organs and develop into a debility or complete loss of vital energy.

These few forces are the main elements for keeping up all vital functions of the body. They provide the body with all necessary substances and energies for healthy function in a complex system of regulation and interplay. Next to the Qi, the two most important elements are essence and mind. The combination of these two words in Chinese actually means vitality or vital power. The combination of the three main forces, Qi, essence, and mind are called the three treasures.

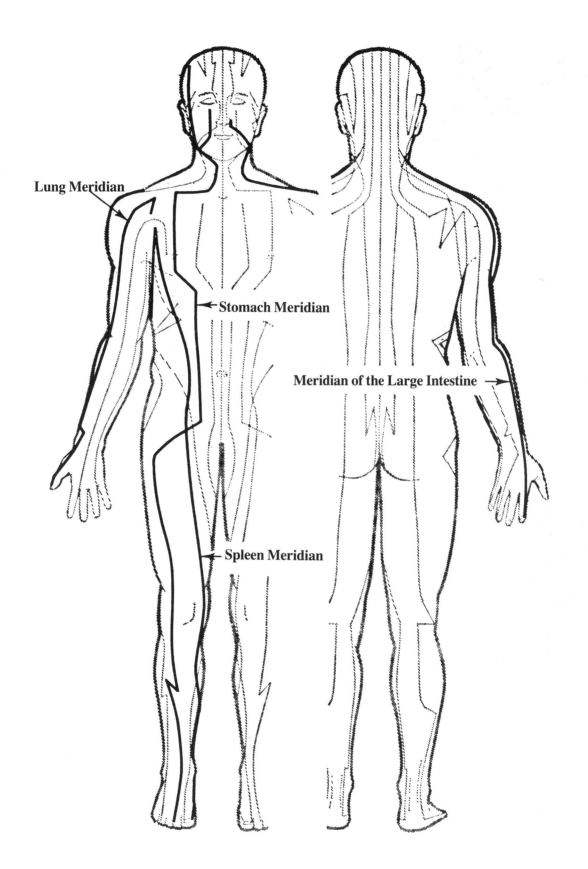

Lung Meridian

Stomach Meridian

Meridian of the Large Intestine

Spleen Meridian

The Meridians

The Qi, the force that keeps up the vital functions of the body, flows through the body along certain channels that can be precisely determined and charted according to certain laws. These channels, or tracks, are called meridians. The meridians constitute the basic system by which Chinese medicine carries out its therapeutic and diagnostic work. There are over two thousand points alongside these meridians that have also been charted and described precisely. These points play a vital role in therapy and diagnosis. They are distributed all over the body on the various meridians.

The most important of the meridians are the twelve main ones, which correspond to the twelve main organs of the body listed above. The twelve main meridians can be found in symmetrical pairs on both sides of the body, one pair of meridians for each organ. Every single point along one of the meridians influences the function of the corresponding organs and is, in turn, influenced by the corresponding organ itself. The various meridians can be detected on the surface of the skin by physical characteristics that are different from the characteristics of the surrounding skin. The most important of these is the fact that every meridian shows a constant rate of electrical resistance along its complete course that is significantly different from the electrical resistance of the bordering parts of the skin.

If this resistance changes from one point to the next, the fact signals a dysfunction of the corresponding organ. Such changes can sometimes be accompanied by increased sensitivity at a particular point, sensitivity that may even result in pain when the point is touched and thereby signals the doctor something is clearly wrong. The acupuncture points along the meridians can also be detected because they have a higher density in the connective tissue below them than do other parts of the skin. If an affliction is healed either through treatment or by the regenerating forces of the body itself, the original state of balance will be repaired, the sensitivity of such a point will disappear, and the rate of electrical resistance will return to normal.

The flow of Qi circulates along the meridians, following a certain course and direction. The final point of the preceding meridian is always close to the starting point of the next. This facilitates the unhindered, continuous flow of Qi until it returns back to the starting meridian, where it is regenerated. We have already heard that the starting point of the circle is the lung meridian. This receives the Qi absorbed from the breath and from food, and successively distributes it over the whole body and into all organs of the body. We will now take a closer look at the different meridians, following the direction that the flow of Qi takes during its course through the meridians.

THE LUNG MERIDIAN

The lung meridian is a Yin meridian. Following the correspondence of elements and organs, the lung meridian belongs to the element metal. It runs from a point above the armpit, down the inside of the arm to the tip of the thumb. The direction of energy flow leads away from the body toward the tip of an extremity. For this reason, the lung meridian is called centripetal. The circulation of Qi always alternates between centrifugal and centripetal meridians. The meridian of the lung receives its energy from the meridian of the liver. The meridian of the lung is used in therapy for lung afflictions such as asthma, bronchitis, and the like, and also for secondary treatment of certain heart diseases. The flow of the Qi moves into the meridian of the large intestine from the lung meridian.

THE MERIDIAN OF THE LARGE INTESTINE

This meridian is classified under the Yang category and, like the lung meridian, belongs to the element metal. Its course is centripetal. Receiving its energy from the lung meridian at the tip of the index finger, this meridian runs up the side of the arm and over the shoulder, then along the collarbone to the side of the neck, from there up the neck and across the jaw, crossing over to the other side of the body over the upper lip, and ending next to the side of the nose.

In therapy this meridian is important in treating diseases of the large intestine as well as, secondarily, afflictions of the teeth or the gums, asthma, and skin diseases. The meridian of the large intestine channels its energy into the stomach meridian.

THE STOMACH MERIDIAN

This meridian is also classified as Yang and belongs to the element earth. It takes a centrifugal course, starting next to the nose and running along the jaw up to the temples, there reverting its direction back to the jaw, then down the neck, crossing the collarbone, and from there straight down the front of the body and the leg, where it ends in the tip of the second toe.

This meridian is important for therapy and diagnosis of diseases of

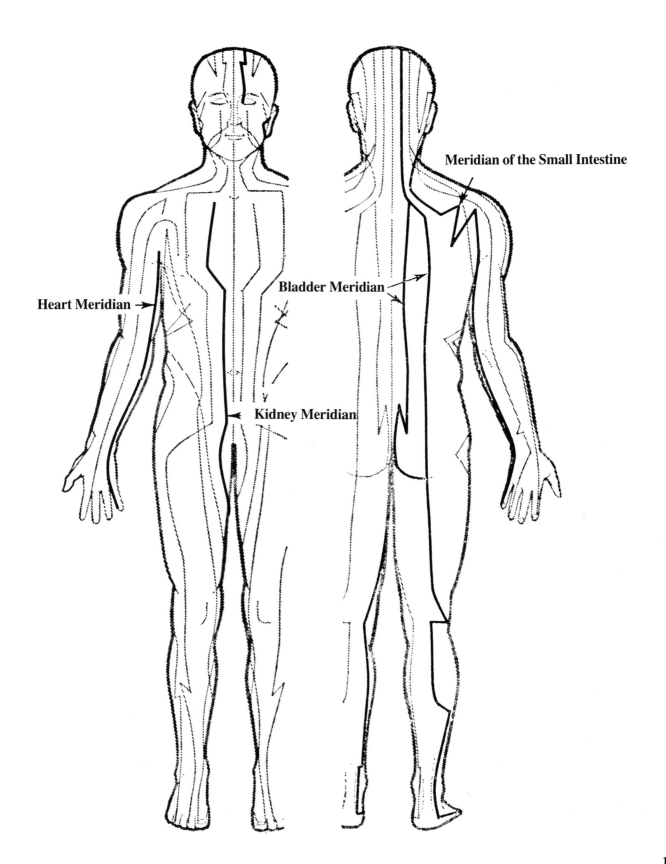

Meridian of the Small Intestine

Bladder Meridian

Heart Meridian

Kidney Meridian

the stomach, but also secondarily for tics, or cramps of the facial muscles and muscles of the neck. The stomach meridian leads into the spleen meridian.

THE SPLEEN MERIDIAN

This meridian is classified as Yin and belongs to the element fire. This meridian runs centripetally, or, in other words, takes the flow of energy towards the direction of the body. It originates at the side of the big toe, from where it leads up the inside of the leg, over the front of the body to a point somewhat above the armpit. There it turns down again, ending on the side of the chest. This meridian is responsible for regulating the digestive system and the sugar metabolism of the body. In addition, it is also important for emotional balance. In China people who are impatient and irritable are often referred to as having "a bad spleen-Qi." This demonstrates how medical insights of this kind have been completely absorbed by popular beliefs.

The spleen meridian is important for treatment of psychical disorders, irritability, and allergic conditions. It releases its energy into the heart meridian.

THE HEART MERIDIAN

This meridian is also classified as Yin and belongs to the element fire. It originates on the thorax, below the pectoral muscle, from where it leads down the inside of the arm to the end of the little finger in a centrifugal direction. Its importance lies mainly in the treatment of heart diseases, but also, indirectly in the treatment of other organs, such as the small intestine, throat, and eyes. It releases its energy into the meridian of the small intestine.

THE MERIDIAN OF THE SMALL INTESTINE

Just as its predecessor, the heart meridian, this meridian belongs to the element fire. It is, however, classified as Yang. Taking over the circulating Qi from the heart meridian, it carries the Qi back toward the center of the body. It originates above the nail of the small finger, extends across the backside of the arm to the height of the shoulder joint, and from there zigzags across the shoulder blade to the height of the first vertebra of the neck. Here it turns towards the front of the body, crossing the side of the neck and jaw, and ending next to the ear.

Besides its significance for diseases of the small intestine, this meridian is also applied in treatment of the stomach, the heart, epilepsy, and Parkinson's disease.

It releases its energy into the bladder meridian.

THE BLADDER MERIDIAN

This meridian is classified as Yang and belongs to the element water. Starting in the inner corner of the eye, it extends up the head and then down again on the back of the body, running parallel to the axis of the body until it reaches the shoulder where it is separated into two strands that follow the same direction down the back at some distance from each other to the small of the back. Here one strand continues down the back of the thigh, while the other runs down the outside of the thigh, until they finally meet again in the hollow of the knee. From there the meridian runs down the back of the leg to the heel and along the outside of the foot to the tip of the little toe. This meridian is important for treatment of cramps, neuralgia, and

rheumatischiagra, and secondarily for treatment of eczema, dysfunctions of the metabolism, and water imbalance in the body.

It releases its energy into the kidney meridian.

THE KIDNEY MERIDIAN

The kidney meridian channels back the energy of the Qi toward the center of the body. It is classified as Yin and belongs to the element water. It originates from a point on the bottom of the foot called "Yong Chuan," which means gushing fountain. This point is important in Easy Tao Exercise 19, where the flow of Qi is stimulated at this point to move up along the leg into the main circulation system of the special meridians, which we will discuss at a later point. From the bottom of the foot, the meridian extends along the inside of the leg to the pubic region, where it almost touches the central axis of the body, and then up the front of the body to the inner end of the collarbone. This meridian can be used for therapy of kidney and heart diseases, as well as for the treatment of neurasthenia and epileptic fits. It releases its energy into the meridian of the pericardium.

THE MERIDIAN OF THE PERICARDIUM

Also called master of the heart, the pericardium meridian is classified as Yin and belongs to the element fire. It originates on the side of the chest between the nipple and the armpit, from where it curves up to the shoulder and down the inside of the arm, where it ends on the tip of the little finger. This meridian and the following triple warmer meridian have a special position in the system of the twelve meridians, since they do not correspond to an actual organ.

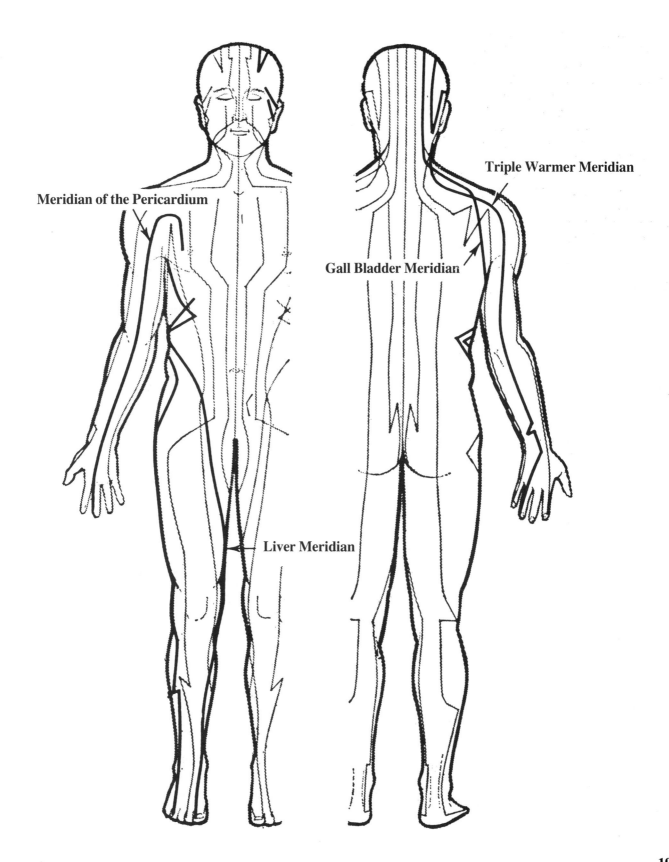

Meridian of the Pericardium

Triple Warmer Meridian

Gall Bladder Meridian

Liver Meridian

Their function is to regulate and govern the interplay of forces of all the other organs and meridians. The main function of the meridian of the pericardium is to harmonize the function of Yin-organs, that is heart, lung, spleen, kidney, and liver. Furthermore it controls the function of oxidation, of the endocrine glands, of the regulation of the amount of blood circulating inside the body, and of the functions of body metabolism. It releases its energy into the triple warmer meridian.

THE TRIPLE WARMER MERIDIAN

Just like the pericardium meridian, the triple warmer belongs to the element fire. It is, however, classified as Yang. Its starting point lies on the tip of the ring finger from where the Qi flows up the backside of the arm, over the shoulder, behind the ear, and on to the temple. From there it turns down toward the jaw, turning up again to end in the outer corner of the eye.

Just as for the previous pericardium meridian, the triple warmer too does not belong to any specific organ. It influences bodily functions such as respiration, digestion, and the urogenital system. It forms a pair of Yin-Yang opposites together with the pericardium meridian, equalizing its functions. In therapy, the triple warmer meridian is used for treatment of breathing disorders, dysfunctions of the digestive system, dysfunctions of the urogenital system, and for neuralgia and deafness. The triple warmer releases its energy into the gall bladder meridian.

THE GALL BLADDER MERIDIAN

This meridian is classified as Yang and takes the flow of Qi back to the extremities of the body in a centrifugal motion. It belongs to the element wood. It originates in the outer corner of the eye, runs across the temple to the back of the head, crosses the shoulder to the front of the body, and then moves down the side of the body, reaching the hip after a double zigzag course. From there stretches down the side of the leg, across the top of the foot, and ends in the tip of the fourth toe. This meridian is used for therapy of migraine, cramps, pain in the lower extremities, and neuralgia. The gall bladder meridian releases its energy into the liver meridian.

ELEMENT	ORGAN	QUALITY	EXTREMITY
Metal	Lung	Yin	Arm
Metal	Large Intestine	Yang	Arm
Earth	Stomach	Yang	Leg
Earth	Spleen	Yin	leg
Fire	Heart	Yin	Arm
Fire	Small Intestine	Yang	Arm
Water	Bladder	Yang	Leg
Water	Kidney	Yin	Leg
Fire	Pericardium	Yin	Arm
Fire	Triple Warmer	Yang	Arm
Wood	Gall Bladder	Yang	leg
Wood	Liver	Yin	leg

THE LIVER MERIDIAN

This meridian closes the circle of Qi that we have been following, flowing across the body and constantly alternating between centrifugal and centripetal movement. The liver meridian is classified as Yin and belongs to the element wood. It originates between the first and second toe. From there it runs up the inside of the leg into the bladder region, then takes a sharp bend outside, and travels in a slow curve to the first ribs on the side of the chest. There it takes another sharp bend and then rises in a straight line to end below the nipple. The liver meridian is important for treatment of disorders of the liver and, additionally of exhaustion, loss of weight, allergies, etc.

These twelve meridians are the vessels for the circulation of the life force Qi, which supplies the body with energy from respiration and from food. Let us have one more final look at the various relations between Yin or Yang quality, location of the meridian, and the corresponding element.

As you can easily see, there is one element for one type of extremity and one Yin and one Yang meridian for each element. At the same time Yin and Yang meridians follow each other in groups of two. This way the elements are always interlocked with each other in the change of Yin and Yang.

Looking at the graphs representing the course of the meridians on the human body, we can see that the meridians do not actually touch each other in their respective ends or starting points, and that in some cases they do not even come close to each other. How then is it possible to assume that there is an unbroken circulation of Qi through all the meridians?

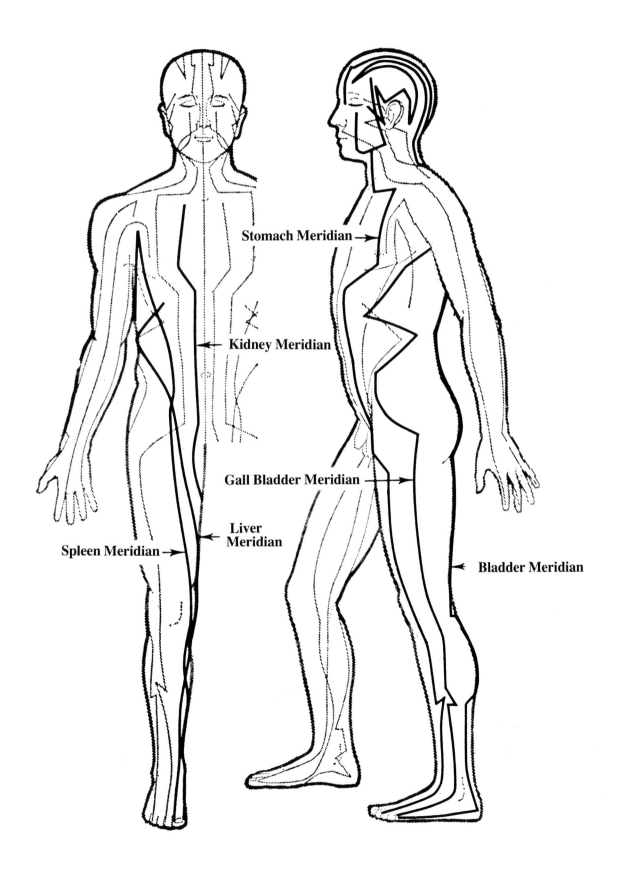

Stomach Meridian →

← Kidney Meridian

Gall Bladder Meridian →

Liver
Meridian

Spleen Meridian →

← Bladder Meridian

The explanation. according to
Chinese medicine, lies in a system of
secondary meridians beyond the
twelve main meridians that we have
so far described. These secondary
meridians constitute a connecting
system between the main meridians.
It would be beyond the scope of this
book on Easy Tao to describe these
secondary systems in detail. However
there is one more system of meridians
whose function is vital for the success
of the exercises of Easy Tao, and we
must therefore take a little look into
the system of special meridians.

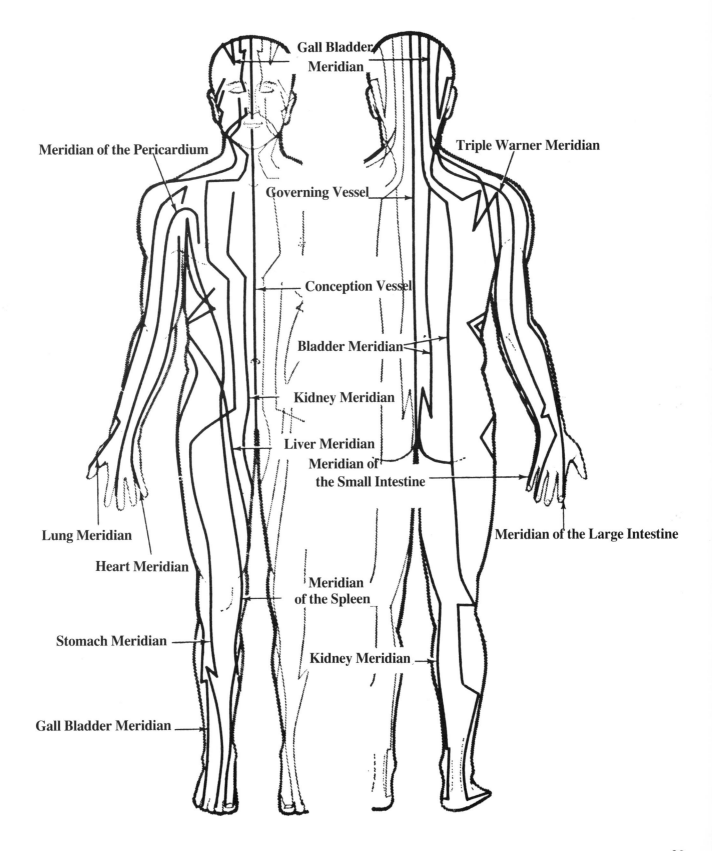

The Special Meridians

THE SPECIAL MERIDIANS

The twelve meridians have already gained widespread acceptance. Even western medicine has conceded that they can be useful in medical therapy. The situation is somewhat different in regard to the special meridians. These channels of energy seem to have no obvious therapeutic value. On top of that, they have always been studied by religious groups and people who wanted to have access to the secret of immortality, a central theme in Chinese philosophy. Such facts make it obvious that traditional western science must find these theories quite hard to swallow.

The theory of the twelve meridians and the theory of the special meridians, however, are based upon the same factual evidence. If one wants to take the trouble to unlock the energies of the special meridians in one's own body, one will soon find that they are not just figments of a vivid imagination.

As we have already mentioned, this secondary system of meridians forms the connection between the twelve main meridians. We will now take a closer look at the two most important of these special meridians.

THE GOVERNING VESSEL

This meridian originates at the point called "Hui Yin," which is located on the symmetry axis of the body between the sexual organs and the anus. From there it rises along the spinal column up the back and neck to the crown of the head, and then back down the forehead and the bridge of the nose to the upper lip, ending inside the mouth above the front teeth. This meridian is classified as Yang.

THE CONCEPTION VESSEL

This meridian is the counterpart of the governing vessel. It originates above the front teeth, right next to the ending point of the governing vessel. From there it traces around the mouth in two branches that join each other again on the chin. Then it runs down the front of the body along the axis that ends between anus and genitals. The flow of energy in this meridian is classified as Yin.

The conception vessel and the governing vessel are the most important of the special meridians, and so we shall say a little about their function. This is essential if we are to understand what Easy Tao is all about. There is no room to detail the several other meridians of secondary function. If we want to use a metaphor for the relation between the twelve body meridians and the two special meridians, we can compare the twelve body meridians to rivers and streams and the two special meridians to the sea. The twelve meridians are important for the transport of energy and for the state of health in the body, but without the two special meridians they could not fulfil their function.

The two special meridians constitute a reservoir of energy and a connecting system for the twelve body meridians, which alone would not have a constantly renewing source of energy to guarantee continuous function of the energy system. The special meridians are, in effect, already in the fetal body in the mother's womb. There they form the circle of rising Yang energies and falling Yin energies, and they constantly balance these two types of energy. This energy system of the embryo that circulates the Qi is in an ideal state of equilibrium and harmony. It is only after birth that this harmony is disturbed and the system becomes less and less able to mix and exchange the polar energies of Yin and Yang. This is because, in daily life, humans are more and more exposed to situations that drain their energy supplies, while not being able to replenish the exhausted energy completely.

Easy Tao gives us the means for halting this constant drain on our natural energy supplies. The exercises make use of certain techniques that can recover the exhausted Qi that has gathered in the extremities, and channel it back to the center of the body and into the original energy system of the two special meridians. When this system is supported and strengthened by further practise of Easy Tao, it can give back its energy to the meridians of the body organs, which will get a supply of fresh, strong Qi. The result of this process is not only a better overall physical condition, but also an improved state of mind and one that is more relaxed and refreshed. It can almost be called a process of rejuvenation. Thus, when you practice Easy Tao, you will become more energetic and more flexible.

One more detail: The two special meridians end and begin at identical points. The circle of energy will, however, only be closed completely when the tongue touches the palate while you are doing the exercises. This way makes it possible to use some secondary channels of energy to completely short-circuit the rising energies of Yang and the sinking energies of Yin in the system of special meridians. The energy then circulates between the two poles—"Bai Hui," the point on the crown of the head, and "Hui Yin," the negative pole on the perineum—and exerts its full rejuvenating, healing effect. This energy is the original force of life. It constitutes the most precious ability of the human body to regenerate itself and to live in perfect harmony with nature.

Tao and Sexuality

The governing and conception vessels constitute the most important energy system of the body, the basis for all other processes of energy exchange in the human body. The importance of this system of energy, which runs from the perineum up the back to the top of the head and down again on the front of the body where it returns to its starting point in the two special meridians along the symmetry axis of the body, does not just lie in the fact that it is connected with the twelve meridians corresponding to the twelve main organs of the body. It also lies in the fact that the energy system of the two special meridians is the key to raising the level of energy in the body and mind as a whole.

Meditation systems of all kinds make use of this system that corresponds to the energy circulation of the unborn baby in the womb receiving its energy directly through the umbilicus. This system works long before the child can receive energy through breathing, which constitutes the most important source of energy from outside after birth.

The system of the two special meridians provides a channel for the original Qi of the former heaven, which can be equated to the fundamental force of life. The main aim of Taoist sages in ancient China was to strengthen this original energy system and make use of its energy. In order to attain this goal, various methods were put to use. Among these were breathing techniques, meditation, and sexual techniques. The importance of sexuality and of sexual energies for the human body was perceived and studied by the Chinese at a very early time. In the oldest works about Chinese medicine, we can already find the basic ideas about sexuality that are still applied today in Chinese medicine.

The exercises that applied the sexual energies to attain better health and to raise the level of mental power were mainly concerned with the energy that lies in the reproductive cells. These cells have the potential of generating human life, which sets them apart from all other cells of the body. In order to produce these life-generating cells, the human body must use up huge amounts of energy and vitality. In other words, to produce the substance that we have called "essence," the body must burn up a lot of Qi energy. As we said earlier, Chinese medicine sees this essence as one of the most important substances of the body, along with mind and Qi. It was therefore only natural for the early Taoists to seek ways of preserving this energy in the body and channelling it back into the system of special meridians.

The duality of Yin and Yang is, of course, applied to sexuality too. The principle of Yang, the rash, hot, fast-moving male principle, is easily excited —but also easily exhausted. The female principle of Yin, however, is quiet, cool and gentle, hard to arouse but also hard to exhaust. These are the fundamental differences between male and female nature as perceived by the Chinese. It seems today that ignorance of the nature of these two principles is causing considerable confusion and frustration in our approach to sexuality.

The Chinese Taoists see sexuality as a possibility for exchange between the subtle, however strong, energies of Yin and Yang, between man and woman. If, however, the nature of male and female sexuality and their different qualities is neglected, the resulting imbalance of energies will cause problems between the two sexes. If every partner looks just for his or her own fulfillment, and if men, especially, do not give their female partners time to arouse their slow Yin energies, but just try to reach orgasm, neither men nor women will ever be able to experience the tremendous inner energies that sexuality can set free. It is therefore important to realize that sexuality can be an exchange of polar energy, wherein each partner receives from the other the kind of energy that is lacking in himself. In this way it is possible to see the differences between the sexes as a great potential for raising one's level of energy and mental awareness, and not as a threat.

One of the main reasons for sexual problems in the West seems to be the preoccupation with having an orgasm, a topic that the Chinese look upon with scepticism and caution. Having observed, in nature, that male animals in a large number of species either die after the sexual act or at least are very exhausted, they have tried to explain this phenomenon with the concept of essence. With these animals it seems that all of their vital energy is used for the purpose of procreation and for the production of reproductive cells. After having fulfilled their purpose, an immense amount of energy is drained from their systems.

It seemed natural, therefore, for the Chinese to look for a way to preserve the vital energy of essence, or semen, inside the body and thus avoid draining it of vital energy again and again. If it were possible to collect the energy of the essence, which in fact is nothing else but finely distilled Qi, and change it back into its original form of Qi, large amounts of energy could be channeled back into the bodily system to benefit the complete organism. The vessel to receive this flow of energy is the special meridian system on the symmetry axis of the body, which can rechannel the recycled energy from the withheld essence into the Qi system of the body. For this reason, the Chinese developed a couple of exercises to keep back this essence and to feed its energy back into the bodily system.

One of these techniques is to contract the muscles of the pelvis and anus so as to block the energy of rising orgasm and to lead the sexual tension in the lower parts of the body, the energy of essence, upwards into the energy system of the special meridians. Easy Tao uses this energy in several exercises where you contract your anal muscles and stimulate the starting point of the system of special meridians, the point "Hui Yin," to make it more receptive for this kind of energy. The exercises of Easy Tao benefit women, too, in helping them to channel their sexual energy into the energy system of the special meridians. But for women, their sexuality being of Yin nature, the problem of keeping the essence does not have the same importance as it does for men.

There is also one simple technique by which men, at least, can keep the essence inside their bodies, while still having orgasms. This technique is to apply pressure on the urethra between the anus and the base of the penis during orgasm, thereby blocking the flow of semen. The semen will not leave the body, but will be channeled into the bladder where it can be reabsorbed by the body. This technique is absolutely harmless and easy to master. Just a few attempts will demonstrate what a man has to pay attention to. This technique is not to be used as a method of contraception, because semen will often be emitted through the penis even before orgasm.

What Chinese Taoists have actually sought to achieve is the abstention from orgasm altogether. They have wanted, instead, to channel their energy of sexual arousal into the special meridian system by way of contractions of muscles or, at a higher state, simply by the power of their mind. This experience is extremely joyful and will raise the mind to ever higher levels of insight, while at the same time giving sexuality a complete new spiritual dimension. All this is achieved by channeling sexual energy, the most powerful and unadulterated kind of Qi. It lets it circulate in the two special meridians, transforming and rejuvenating body and mind.

The Eight Introductory Exercises

The Preparatory Exercises

The first eight lessons serve as a preparation.
They are essential to the whole method of Easy Tao.

You should use these lessons for warm up.
And when you feel you have mastered them, you can advance
to the next twelve exercises.

The measure of success is your own experience of Qi.
Each lesson should be performed without any strain.
Stretching, deep breathing,
and correct posture
are at the center of every lesson.

The First Exercise

Embracing the Moon

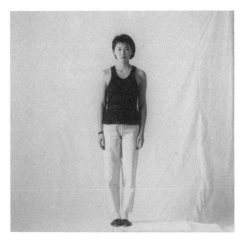

The end position for every exercise

consists of the two meridians, the governing and receiving vessels. Standing in this position, raise the hands up to the navel, palms facing up and the left hand placed on top of the right. The two thumbs touch at the thumb tips. Remain still in this position for a few seconds and try to relax your mind.

Then move the stretched arms in a circular motion up above the head and hold the palms pointed upward horizontally, with fingertips touching each other. Simultaneously, bend your neck backwards and look at your hands. During this movement inhale through the nose. The mouth remains closed. As you are breathing

The hands held together in front of the stomach

Start this exercise standing with heels touching each other and the tips of the feet pointing outward. The legs and the back are straight, and the body should be relaxed. The head is upright, looking straight ahead. Lips are closed and the teeth touch

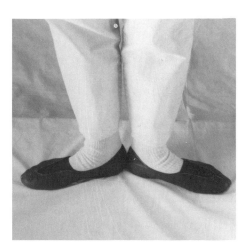

The toes point outward, the heels touch one another

Slowly move the arms in an upward circle

slightly. The tongue touches the top of the palate to close the energy circuit along the axis of the body that

Embracing the Moon

in, concentrate on the air filling up your lungs completely and try to emit the sound "hng" from the "Dan Tian" point, which is located about an inch below the navel. After a few seconds, move your hands back to their original position in front of the abdomen. At the same time, breathe out slowly and concentrate on the Qi that you have taken up with your breath flowing into the Dan Tian point. Exhaling the air generates a sound like "ha" that arises from this point as well

This exercise is repeated three times.

Remain in this position for a few seconds before letting the arms down in front of the stomach again

SUMMARY OF EXERCISE ONE

"EMBRACING THE MOON"

Stand with feet pointing outward.

Put hands in front of the abdomen, palms pointing upwards.

Raise hands above the head with outstretched arms.

Keep eyes looking ahead, following the motion of the arms above the head and back down again.

Breathe audibly through the nose.

While inhaling, picture the Qi rising in the chest; while exhaling, picture it sinking into the Dan Tian point.

Embracing the Moon

The Second Exercise

Turning the Head

Again in the final position

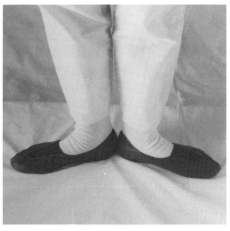

Keep feet in as straight a line as possible

The arms outstretched and the hands pointed upward

This exercise begins in the same position as the first. The tips of the toes point away from each other. The heels touch each other. The legs and the body are straight and relaxed. The back can be slightly bent forward, but the chest should not be thrust outward. The head points straight ahead. The mouth is closed, the teeth touch slightly. The tongue touches the top of the palate closing the energy circuit on the axis of the

body. The arms hang by the side of the body.

Raise both arms simultaneously and extend them away from the body at shoulder level. The palms point outwards and the hands are flexed up. Rotate the head to the left and focus your eyes at the tip of the middle finger for about twenty seconds. At the same time concentrate on the Qi that is

generated at the tip of the middle finger. This point is the originating point for one of the acupuncture meridians, the vessels which transport the vital force of Qi through the body. When you just start practising Easy Tao, it might not immediately be possible to actually feel the Qi that is generated in the exercises. This takes a special kind of sensibility that is only acquired through patient, continuous practice.

Concentrate on the middle finger of the left hand. . .

. . .then on the right hand

The body remains facing forward

Turning the Head

You will sense a certain tingling sensation, a kind of vibration in the corresponding part of the body.

After fixing your eyes on the middle finger of the left hand, do likewise with your right hand, focusing on the middle finger and concentrating on the Qi arising from the tip of the finger.

SUMMARY OF EXERCISE TWO

"TURNING THE HEAD"

Stand with feet on one line, heels touching.

Extend arms to the side of the body at shoulder level.

Point palms outwards, finger-tips upwards.

Rotate the head first left and then right, focusing each time for about twenty seconds on the middle finger of the corresponding hand.

Turning the Head

The Third Exercise

Walking on Ice

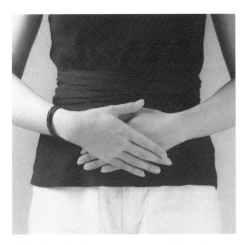

The hands lie over one another in front of the stomach

Spread your legs slightly

Upper body forward and a small step to the right. . .

Place your feet about one foot apart from each other, pointing forward and resting firmly on the floor. Your hands are placed on top of each other on the lower part of the abdomen, about two fingers below the navel, with the right hand on top of the left. The back and your head is straight, eyes gazing forward. Close the energy circuit on the middle axis of the body by placing the tongue on the roof of the mouth. The lips are closed, and the teeth touch slightly.

Then, without raising the foot, move the right foot forward about a half step. Simultaneously, bend your body forward a little, with your back remaining straight. Inhale through your nose. The air flowing in through the nose should make an audible sound, sounding somewhat like "hng." With your hands remaining in the position above the abdomen, concentrate on the Qi rising from that part of the abdomen and going into the back. Then raise your body to the upright position again and exhale with a slightly opened mouth. The air should again make an audible sound somewhat resembling the syllable

"ha." At the same time, concentrate on the Qi flowing from the back into the lower part of the abdomen. Pull your right foot back again into the starting position.

Then put your left hand on top of the right hand on the lower part of the abdomen and repeat the same motion with the left foot. Repeat the entire

exercise three times. When you have completed the exercise, let your hands hang loosely at the sides of your body.

. . .then to the left—and stand up straight again

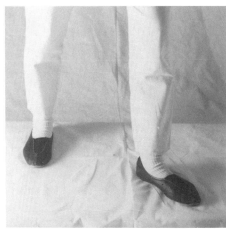

The foot should not be lifted from the floor

SUMMARY OF EXERCISE THREE

"WALKING ON ICE"

Place the legs slightly apart, toes pointing forward.

Place the hands on top of each other on the lower part of the abdomen.

Take a step forward with the right foot in an angle of about 45 degrees; the bottom of the foot remains touching the floor.

At the same time bend your body forward slightly and inhale slowly, making an audible sound.

Pull the foot back into original position and raise the body, exhaling slowly and audibly.

Repeat with the other foot. Do three sets each, alternating feet.

Walking on Ice

The Fourth Exercise

Raising the Arms

Spread your legs apart

Bend your knees slightly. . .

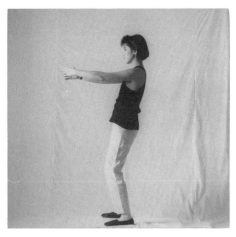

. . .move your arms upward in a half circle. . .

Place your feet apart with the insteps approximately in line with the shoulders. Your body should be straight and relaxed, the shoulders loose. The head is straight, looking forward. The energy circuit on the middle axis of the body is closed with the tongue placed on the top of the mouth. Raise your arms in front of your body, with your fingers relaxed and your palms facing each other.

Now turn your head to the left as far back as possible and at the same time raise your arms above your head. As you do this, breathe out with the air making a sound like "ha." Then lower the arms in front of the body. Repeat three times. Next raise the arms straight above the head and concentrate for about half a minute on the Qi flowing into the tips of the fingers. Repeat with the head turning

right this time, also breathing audibly. After three movements, raise the arms and concentrate on the Qi in the fingertips. At the end of the exercise, lower the arms until the hands rest by the side of the thighs, relaxing for a few seconds before you start the next exercise.

. . .behind the head

Turn head first to the left. . .

. . .and then to the right

Raising the Arms

SUMMARY OF EXERCISE FOUR

"RAISING THE ARMS"

Stand with your legs apart at shoulder width.

Raise arms in front of the body, palms facing each other.

Turn head back to the left, raising arms in a circular motion at the same time.

Breathe out audibly, but slowly.

Lower arms back in front of body.

Repeat three times, then hold arms up for a half a minute concentrating on the Qi in your fingertips.

Repeat on the other side.

Raising the Arms

The Fifth Exercise

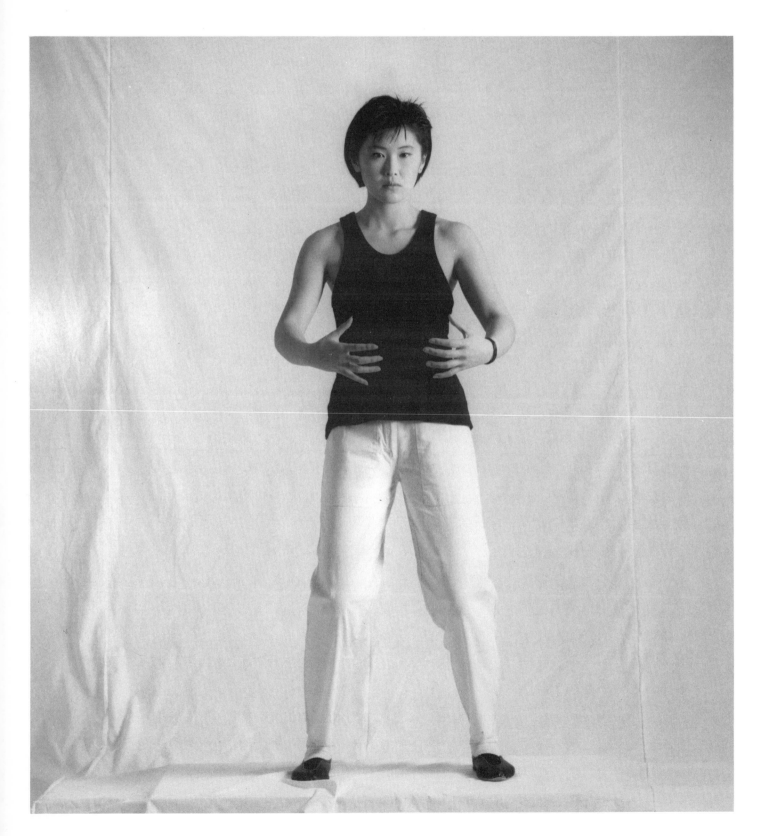

Embracing the Basket

Spread your legs apart and bend your knees slightly

. . .as if you had a basket in your hands

Upper body turned to the left. . .

Start from the same position as you did in exercise four, facing the front with legs bent slightly at the knee. The body should be upright, the head straight. The energy circuit on the middle axis is closed by the tongue touching the top of the mouth. Concentrate on the point of gravity in your body, which should be felt in the feet. The arms are placed in front of the body with the elbows bent, as if you were holding a very large basket. The fingers are straight and relaxed. Relax the shoulders and thighs completely, and position the knees forward slightly vertically above the feet. It is important, however, that the knees do not protrude beyond the vertical line rising from the toes of your feet.

Then start turning the body from the hip, 90 degrees to the left. Then turn to the right. The only moving part of the body is the hip area. All other parts— the arms, legs, feet—do not move from their original position. The feet must remain firmly on the floor. It is very important that the chest remains relaxed and loose, so that the breath can flow freely. Rotate the body nine times to each side.

. . .and then turn to the right

The arms remain loosely outstretched

Then lower the arms to the side of the body, and take a step inwards so that the feet touch.

**"EMBRACING THE BAS-
KET"**

Stand with legs placed apart.

Raise arms in front of the body
with the elbows bent slightly,
as if holding a very large basket.

Turn body left and right nine
times, moving from the hip.

Embracing the Basket

Bending the Body

Spread your legs apart, make a fist

Stand with your legs apart, feet at about shoulder width and parallel to each other, toes pointing forward. The legs, as well as the body, are stretched and straight, with the whole body in a relaxed state. The chest should not protrude in an unnatural manner. The back can be slightly bent. Also, do not tense the shoulders. They should be loose and relaxed. The head is straight and upright facing forward. The main energy circuit on the axis of the body is closed with the tongue touching the top of the mouth. Breathe slowly and naturally; the whole body is completely relaxed. Your hands, which hang by the sides of your thighs, form hollow fists with the thumb on the outside.

Now bend the body forward and touch the ground in front of the left foot with your left fist. The "eye" of the fist, that is the hollow that is formed between thumb and index fingers, should be pointing forward. If you cannot bend your body far enough, then you need not try to touch the ground. Just make sure that the knees remain stretched all through this exercise. While touching the ground with your left fist, the right fist remains at about knee level. While bending the body forward, the head remains raised and the eyes should remain focused to the front. While bending down, exhale slowly but forcefully with the outgoing air generating a sound like "ha." Then raise the body again and return to the original position, at the same time breathing in and generating the sound "hng" in your nose as the air passes through it. Repeat the exercise three times with left hand and right hand alternately.

And exactly the same on the other side

The left fist touches the left foot. . .

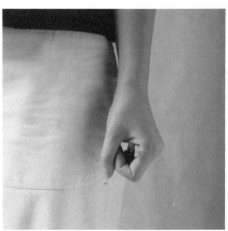

The opening of the hole in the fist faces forward

51

Bending the Body

SUMMARY OF EXERCISE SIX

"BENDING THE BODY"

Stand with legs placed apart from each other at shoulder width.

Let arms hang down by the side of the body, hands forming hollow "fists."

Bend body forward and touch the ground in front of left foot with left hand, knees remaining stretched.

When bending forward, exhale slowly but audibly.

Raise body, at the same time breathing in slowly but audibly.

Repeat with the other hand, three times each.

Bending the Body

The Seventh Exercise

Harvesting Rice

Spread your legs, and make a fist

In a deep crouch

Stand with your legs slightly apart. The legs should be straight, the body upright. But your chest should not be thrust outward unnaturally. Your head should be upright and facing forward. The whole body should be relaxed and loose, the breath quiet and relaxed. The tongue touches the top of the mouth, thereby closing the energy circuit along the middle axis of the body. From this position bend the body forward, at the same time bending your knees until the elbows are at knee level and the fingers touch the top of your feet. While bending down, breathe in evenly and forcefully enough for it to make a slight sound as the air passes through your nose.

From this crouching position, put your left foot to the side, shifting the weight to the left foot. Then start raising your head, with your eyes looking forward, and raise your body. At the same time, raise your left arm straight into the air in a vertical motion by the side of your ear. The palm should be facing outward. Your right hand is placed on your hip and then stretched downward as you raise your body. When you are standing up, breathe

Step to the left with the left arm raised

The right hand will be stretching downward

The end point of the movement

The palm of the outstretched hand turned inward

out letting the air make a slight sound like "'ha" when it passes through your mouth. Then return your foot to its original position, and do the same exercise with the right hand. Repeat, left and right each three times.

The open fist

SUMMARY OF EXERCISE SEVEN

"HARVESTING RICE"

Stand with legs placed slightly apart.

Let your arms hang at the sides of the body.

Bend your body and knees, with elbows at knee level and arms hanging loosely at the sides of the body. Hands touch the top of the feet.

Bend down, take a small step to the side with the left foot, and raise your head. At the same time breathe in audibly.

Raise body and stretch legs.

While standing, the left hand is stretched above the head, the right hand is stretched downward from the hip. At the same time, exhale audibly through the mouth.

Return the left foot to its original position and repeat on the other side.

Harvesting Rice

The Eighth Exercise

Bending the Back

Relaxed, spread your legs slightly apart

Arms over your head, upper body bent back

The end position for the side

Arms in front. . .

. . .raise them over your head. . .

. . .and follow your hands with your eyes

Stand with legs slightly apart, knees slightly bent, head straight, eyes straight ahead. The tongue is touching the top of the mouth, thereby closing the energy circuit on the middle axis of the body. The arms hang relaxed at the sides of the body. Then slowly move the hands, raising them horizontally in front of the body and further up over the head to a position as far behind the head as possible. At the same time bend backwards and follow the movement of the hands with the head. While doing this, breathe in steadily, with the air making a small hissing sound as it fills the lungs. While breathing in, concentrate on the Qi flowing from the lower part of the abdomen into the lungs. Next start to reverse the movement, raising your back and lowering your arms in front on your chest, at the same time breathing out steadily and strongly. The air flowing out of the lungs makes a sound like "ha." Concentrate on the Qi flowing from the back of the chest into the lower part of the abdomen. Now bend the knees slightly and start all over again. Repeat three times.

Bending the Back

Bending the Back

Main Exercises

If you have mastered the first eight lessons,
you are now ready for the next twelve.

It is highly recommended that you spend
additional effort on the first
eight lessons before you move on
to the next lessons of Easy Tao,
if it has been a long time
since you exercised regularly
or participated in strenuous sports activities.

In any case, you must practice every day
for as long as an hour to get the fullest benefits
from these advanced exercises.

You may not be able to perceive new effects
from day to day.
But you will experience significant new energy
with the passage of time.
And your singleness of purpose
in the pursuit of this Chinese way to health
will manifest itself in many other aspects of your life.

The Ninth Exercise

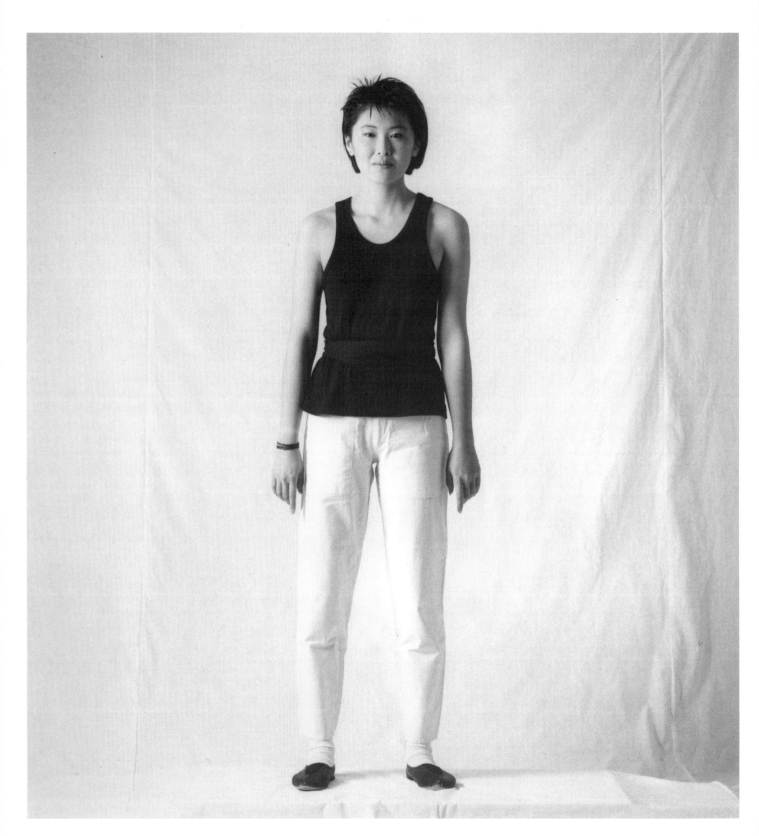

Searching for Relaxation

The view to the front—legs slightly apart

Complete relaxation

middle finger stretched slightly outward. The head is straight, with eyes facing the front. The point "Bai Hui" at the top of the head must be completely calm and firm. You should have a feeling that the entire body is fixed on this point.

Breathe easily and evenly through your nose. The mouth is closed and the teeth are slightly clenched. The tongue lies on the upper palate, shutting off the circulation of energy between the two meridians along the axis of symmetry of your body.

Your mind should be calm. Try to abandon all thoughts. Concentrate only on your body and this exercise. Stand still in this position and, with the aid of your breathing (the "outer Qi"), wait for the pulsation of the inner Qi. Do not become impatient or uneasy. Relax and think about how the energy of your breathing can bring out the energy within your body.

After a while, you will start to feel the power of Qi at your finger-tips. It first begins with a prickling sensation or a feeling of warmth, which gradually increases to an actual shaking of the fingers. Then, with your mind lead this power to your lower and upper arms, all the way to your shoulders.

Gentle vibrations should start to take place in your arms and shoulders, increasing in intensity until these respective parts of your body begin to actually shake. Once these strong vibrations have set in, it is a sign that the invigorating power of Qi has spread and expanded its stimulating effect to your entire body. You can control this shaking or stop it completely by tensing your arm muscles, if you feel uncomfortable. However these vibrations are basically the most important part of

Fingers outstretched, back of the hand facing front

these exercises, and you should try to gradually become used to them.

If the vibrations do not come automatically in the beginning, you can swing your arms slightly, starting from the shoulders. You will then notice a rhythm in the prickling sensation of your fingertips and in the inner pulsations, which have been brought about by your shaking.

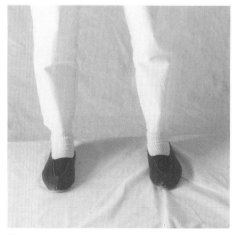

The feet firm on the ground

Begin this exercise by facing east. This is because Chinese people are used to exercising early in the morning while facing the rising sun. Stand in the starting position with the legs slightly apart. Place your feet firmly on the ground. Your whole body should be straight and relaxed, with arms hanging loosely and placed alongside the upper thighs. The backs of your hands face the front, with the

Exercise Nine can be carried out for several minutes. If you have rheumatic pains in your arms or shoulders, you can use your own will to lead this power of Qi to those places, and thus relieve and even heal the pains. Exercise Nine calms your mind and strengthens the vitality of your body.

SUMMARY OF EXERCISE NINE

"SEARCHING FOR RELAXATION"

Stand with your legs slightly apart.

Your arms hang at the sides of your body, fingers stretched, and the backs of the hands face the front.

Relax in this position and wait for the Qi, which starts to vibrate in the fingertips, leading to stronger vibrations in your hands, arms, and shoulders.

Searching for Relaxation

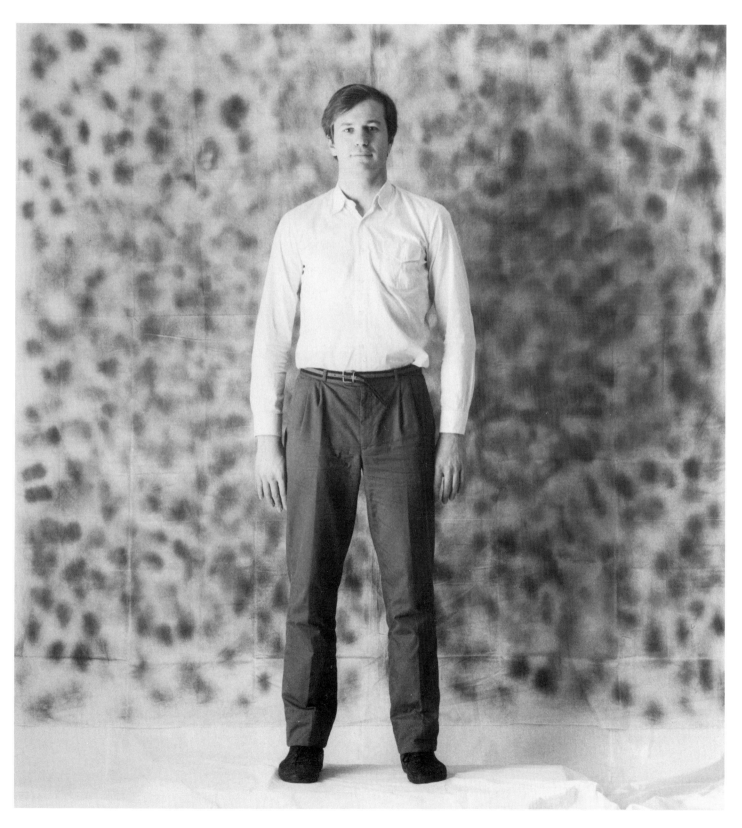

The Tenth Exercise

Breathing Like a Turtle

Legs slightly apart at the beginning

Begin this exercise in the usual starting position, with legs slightly apart. Stand, facing east, with your body upright and straight. The feet remain firmly flat on the floor. The neck, however, is stretched slightly forward, resembling the position of a turtle's neck.

The Chinese are close observers of nature, and in many exercises tend to breathe in the same manner as animals that possess certain attributes.

The turtle is a main Chinese symbol of longevity—a goal especially worth striving for. The Chinese try to share in the turtle's energy through imitation.

Breathing has a special meaning in this exercise, as it transforms the Qi of nature into the Qi of the body.

During this exercise your mouth is closed, and your teeth are slightly clenched. Your tongue lies on the upper palate in order to close the circulation of energy of the two main meridians. The point "Bai Hui" will

be lifted slightly by the stretching of the neck.

Both hands are placed on the lower part of the abdomen—the right hand over the left—around two fingers-width beneath the navel.

As you inhale slowly and evenly—without a break—through the nose, slightly lean the upper torso backwards, with the back remaining straight and the neck stretched a little forward. At the same time, the muscles of the anus are pulled upward. This activates one of the most important energy centers: the point "Hui Yin" on the perineum between the anus and the genitals, which functions as the pump for the circulation of energy in the body.

Concentrate on the air you inhale so that it reaches the bottom of your abdomen. You should be able to feel how your abdomen arches like a small drum.

Once you have inhaled completely, lean straight forward with your upper torso. Stretch out your neck

Hands: overlapping on the lower part of the stomach

and exhale, slowly and evenly without a break. Imagine that the vertex "Bai Hui" is leaning on an object. The muscles of the anus can be relaxed during exhalation. After exhaling, start straightening your body, and inhale when the upper torso is halfway straight. Both inhalation and exhalation should take about 30 seconds each.

When bending forward, the neck will be stretched slightly upward

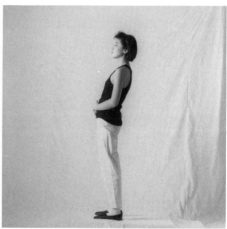

Slowly breathe in while bending back the upper body. . .

Breathing Like a Turtle

. . .and slowly breathe out while bending forward

Then stand up again

Repeat this exercise nine times. Apart from the fact that your chest and belly are relaxed and your spirit and body feel free and refreshed, the main effect of this exercise is the stimulation of the "inner breathing" of your body.

If you practice this exercise regularly for an extended period of time, you will feel as if the pores of your skin and the "Bai Hui" vertex can breathe. This is an indication that the circulation of Qi in your entire body is being strengthened and intensified.

The hands lie in front of the stomach

Breathing Like a Turtle

The Eleventh Exercise

Swinging Your Arms

Stretch your legs far apart

Bend your knees slightly

Press the edge of the hand between the thumb and the forefinger—first with the left on the right. . .

Begin again in the starting position, but with your feet a little wider apart. Bend your legs only to the extent where you can stand in that position for a period of time without straining yourself.

The upper torso should be upright and relaxed, rather than unnaturally tense. Hold your head straight so that your eyes look forward. Your mouth should be closed and your teeth

slightly clenched. The tongue lies on the upper palate and thus shuts off the circulation of energy of the two meridians along the axis of symmetry in the body. The back of your head and your buttocks form a vertical line.

Raise your left arm to your chest. Bend the elbow slightly and relax the left arm while opening your fingers. The fingertips are pointed forward

and the palm is open to the right.

With the side of the right hand, press the point called "Hu Kou," which lies between the thumb and index finger of the left hand. "Hu Kou" is the starting point of a meridian, and its energy is stimulated by this pressure.

Press this point for about 10 seconds, then change hands. Now press the "Hu Kou" of the right hand with the

. . .then right on the left

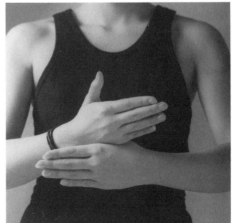

Press the edge of the hand in this position

The arms outstretched in front of the body

Swinging Your Arms

Bend the upper body forward without bending knees—the arms facing backwards. . .

. . .then bend deeply—and bend the arms forward again

While throwing the arms forward, bend the knees deeply

side of the left hand.

Then stretch both arms out so that they are parallel to each other and perpendicular to the body. Bend the upper torso forward 90 degrees. Straighten and stretch the legs, and then gently swing the arms to the back alongside the body. Face the palms upward and also stretch the fingers in this direction. Imagine that

the vertex point, "Bai Hui," is leaning on an object.

Next move into a squatting position, and with the momentum of this action, swing the arms to the front. This movement involves only the hands and arms; the rest of the body remains completely relaxed.

Repeat this exercise nine times. First

stretch the legs, bend forward and swing the arms to the back. Then squat and swing the arms to the front.

Stay in this squatting position with outstretched hands, palms facing down, and wait patiently for the Qi vibration in the fingertips. You will feel the vibration from your hands all the way to your shoulders. This can

Swing the arms upward. . .

. . .and lift the body up again. . .

. . .until you return to the original position

Swinging Your Arms

Then bend forward again

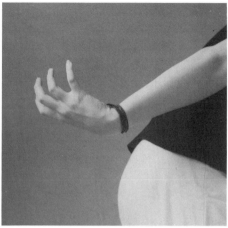

Close the hands forty-nine times. . .

. . .and open them again

be very refreshing and stimulating.

After one to two minutes, stretch the knees again and bend the upper torso forward. The arms are placed next to the body with the palms facing upward. In this position, wait again for the tingling sensation from the hands to move all the way up in your arms.

The eleventh exercise strengthens and refreshes the entire body and provides relief for the fatigue, exhaustion, and backaches.

Again in the end position

Close the hands forty-nine times. . .

. . .and stretch out again

Swinging Your Arms

SUMMARY OF
EXERCISE ELEVEN

"SWINGING YOUR ARMS"

Squat with legs apart.

Lift the arms horizontally to the front of the chest.

Press the curve between the thumb and the index finger of the left hand with the edge of the right hand for a few seconds, and then repeat with the other hand.

Stretch the legs and bend the upper torso 90 degrees.

Place arms on both sides of the body and point the hands upwards.

From a low squatting position, swing the arms alongside the body towards the front and slowly raise the upper torso so that, at the end of this movement, you are again standing

slightly squatted with arms stretched in front of the chest.

Again from a low squatting position, swing the arms towards the back until you are in the starting position with stretched legs, bent upper torso, and arms on both sides of the body. This movement should be repeated nine times.

Stand relaxed, with arms in front of the chest, and wait for the Qi to begin to vibrate in your fingertips. This vibration will then generate stronger vibrations in the arms and shoulders.

Bend the body forward again, with arms next to the body as in the starting position, and again wait for the Qi in your fingertips, which then spreads to the arms and shoulders.

Swinging Your Arms

The Twelfth Exercise

Flapping Your Wings

Spread your legs slightly

Begin this exercise in a relaxed starting position, with legs straight and slightly apart, the head facing the front. Your whole body should be fixed on the vertex "Bai Hui" at the top of the head. The mouth is closed and the teeth are slightly clenched. The tongue lies on the upper palate in order to close the circulation of energy of the two main meridians. The shoulders are completely

Hands folded with outstretched arms in front of the body

relaxed, and the arms hang down loosely on each side of the body.

First, stretch out your arms horizontally to the front, with palms touching each other. Then turn the palms upward and extend your arms horizontally to each side so that they are in line with the shoulders. The hands are open and the fingers stretched.

Now lift your toes off the ground. Once in this position, gently bring your fingers together and then stretch them out again. Your hands should be arched outward when stretching.

Repeat this movement at least nine times. Depending on your physical condition, this exercise can be repeated 49 times.

Stand then with arms stretched to the side and your toes lifted, waiting calmly for the vibration of Qi in your fingertips. With your willpower, you can move this prickling feeling from the arms to the shoulders, until you sense a vibration from the shoulders all the way back to the arms.

If, at the beginning, you cannot immediately sense the prickling feeling of Qi, don't be impatient. It can take awhile for the Qi to make itself noticeable. Even if you don't feel it, the Qi is there and has its effect in different ways, depending on the person.

If you don't feel the power of Qi strongly enough in the beginning, you can try to swing your arms to support the effect of the gentle prickling of Qi. While doing this, you will discover the best way to feel the effect of Qi for yourself. Depending on your physical condition, you can swing your arms as long as you want—up to several minutes. If you feel that the

Arms outstretched with the palm of the hands upward

vibrations have become too strong, you can control their intensity by tensing your muscles.

Stretch the hands completely forty-nine times. . .

. . .and close gently

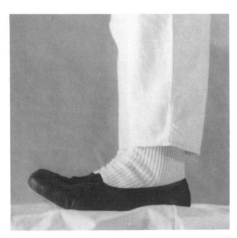

The toes remain pointed upward

SUMMARY OF EXERCISE TWELVE

"FLAPPING YOUR WINGS"

Stand with the legs slightly apart.

Stretch your arms sideways to shoulder height, with palms facing upward. Lift the toes.

Relax, and then stretch your fingers outwards, up to 49 times.

Wait for the Qi to start vibrating from your fingertips into the arms and up to your shoulders.

Flapping Your Wings

The Thirteenth Exercise

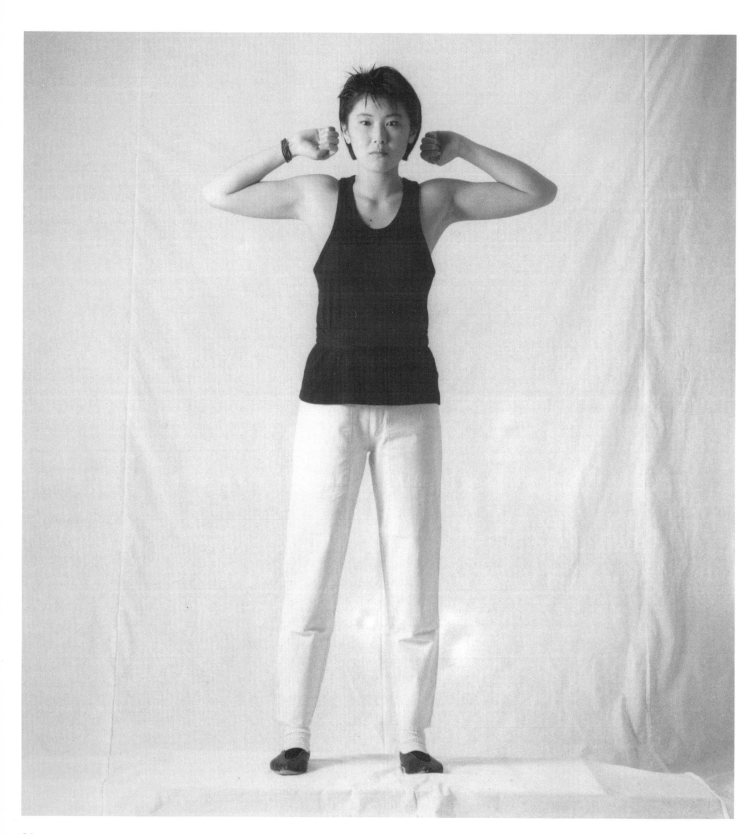

Spread your legs slightly, arms stretched to the side

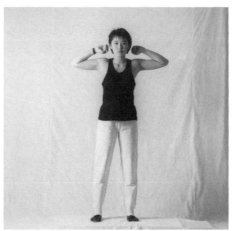

With arms bent, make a fist

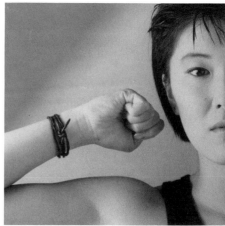

Press the fists together forty-nine times. . .

Stand with your legs slightly apart. Your body should be straight and relaxed. Eyes should face front. The head should be upright.

The mouth is closed and the teeth are lightly clenched. The tongue lies on the upper palate in order to close the circulation of energy of the two main meridians.

The shoulders are also relaxed. You should start this exercise with a feeling that the whole body is fixed on the vertex "Bai Hui."

The arms, which were stretched out horizontally to each side of the body in Exercise Twelve, should now be bent at the elbows, with each hand forming a fist and the fingers covering the thumb.

The fists should be at ear-level, directly over the pit formed by the collar-bone and the shoulder muscles.

Begin now to tighten the fists. Then relax them. While doing this, the elbows should not move, and be sure that the shoulders are not tensed involuntarily. The arms and shoulders should remain completely relaxed. The only movement and

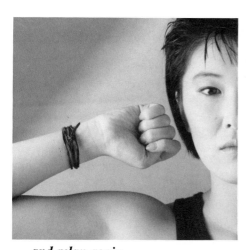

. . .and relax again

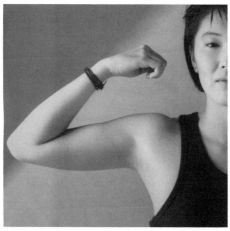

When the Qi flows, begin to circle the lower arm next to the ear

Rotating Your Fists

If you cannot feel the effect of Qi in the beginning, you can call forth the vibrations yourself. But be sure that the vibrations of Qi are induced slowly.

exertion should be in the fists, which are turned a little to the front while being tensed.

Altogether, Exercise Thirteen should be repeated 49 times. The number of repetitions completed will depend on your physical condition. The Chinese always try to do exercises in multiples of nine.

Remain in this position without moving. The body is now again totally relaxed; your breathing is calm and even. Wait for the Qi to start prickling in your fists. When the vibration increases, the fists will begin to rotate next to your ears. As the vibration increases even more, the movement will extend from the fists to the lower arms, causing them to rotate and in turn causing the fists to rotate in even larger circles next to the ears.

The vibration continues in the shoulders, the chest, and the back. The intensity and length can be set and controlled by tensing the muscles involved.

SUMMARY OF EXERCISE THIRTEEN

"ROTATING YOUR FISTS"

Stand with your legs slightly apart.

Form two fists with your hands, fingers over the thumbs.

The upper arms should be in line with your shoulders and stretched at the sides of your the body.

The elbows should be bent.

The fists are then placed over the pit between the shoulder muscles and collar-bone.

Wait in this position for the Qi to set the fists and lower arms in motion, rotating in circles next to the ear.

84

Rotating Your Fists

The Fourteenth Exercise

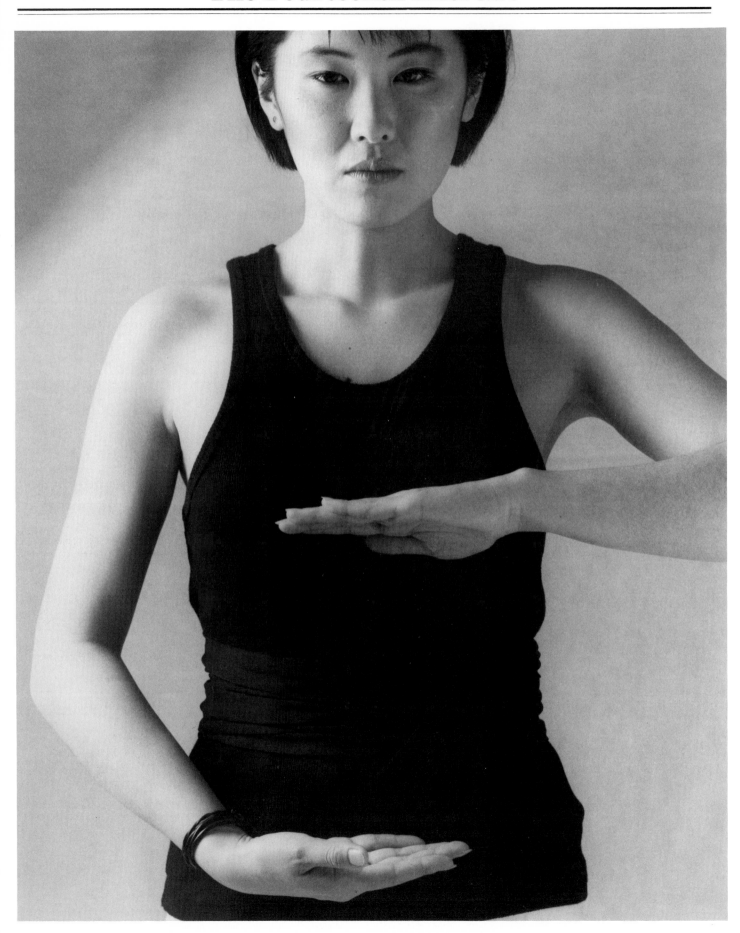

The Equilibrium Between Heaven and Earth

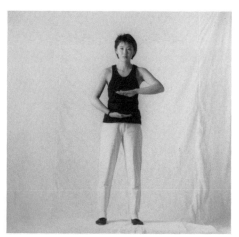

One hand in front of the chest, one in front of the abdomen

Slowly move one hand up and one hand down...

. . .until the left is over the head and the right is near the thigh

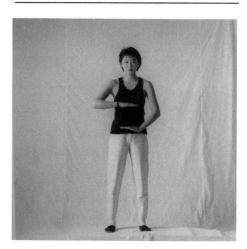

The hands are reversed. . .

. . .and go slowly above and below again. . .

symmetry of your body. Now place both hands in front of your body, with the left hand at the height of your heart and the right just below your navel. The palms should face each other horizontally.

Lift the left hand slowly upward along the central axis of your body until it is over your head. Follow this movement with your eyes and bend your head slightly back. Now stretch your left arm, bending back the left hand so it is perpendicular to the arm and leave it in this horizontal position. The fingers are outstretched and opened, with the index finger pointing to the back of the hand. The tip of your middle finger should now be directly above the vertex "Bai Hui."

As you move the left hand up, press the right hand down until the right thumb reaches the right thigh. The fingers of this hand are stretched and relaxed— and the index finger is slightly lifted.

When you have reached this position, close both hands as if you were

Begin by standing in the usual starting position, facing east. Take a small step to the left, and stand with your legs slightly apart. Your feet should be firmly on the floor, with the upper torso straight, upright, and relaxed. Look straight forward. Your mouth should be closed and your teeth slightly clenched. Your tongue lies on the upper palate, shutting off the circulation of energy between the two meridians along the axis of

grasping something. Now open your hands all the way so that the fingers form a tight arch with the back of your hands. This opening and closing process should be repeated 36 times. If this is too much, choose a lower multiple of "nine." Now stay in this position—left arm stretched over your head, right arm stretched along the body—and wait until you feel the power of Qi in your fingertips. The vibration will start in your hands and

The Equilibrium Between Heaven and Earth

. . .until the end position

Stretch the lower hand forty-nine times. . .

. . .and slowly close

At the same time stretch the upper hand forty-nine times. . .

...and slowly close

arms and become strong, regular pulsations. Let the effect of the power of Qi last a couple of minutes and check its intensity by contracting your muscles. Next, repeat the exercise with the right hand in front of your heart and the left below your navel. The right hand will now be lifted upward over the head, the left downward to the left thigh. This exercise loosens up and relaxes your chest and promotes the functioning of your digestive organs.

SUMMARY OF EXERCISE FOURTEEN

"THE EQUILIBRIUM BETWEEN HEAVEN AND EARTH"

Stand with your legs spread slightly.

The left hand held horizontally in front of the chest, with the palm facing downward.

The right hand held horizontally in front of the abdomen, palm facing upward.

Raise the left hand vertically over your head, with the fingers slightly bent and pointing upward.

At the same time, lower the right hand along your body until it reaches the upper thigh.

In this position, tense and then relax the fingers up to 36 times.

Wait for the vibration of Qi, which begins in the fingertips and rises to the arms and shoulders.

Repeat this exercise with the arms in the opposite position.

The Equilibrium Between Heaven and Earth

The Fifteenth Exercise

Crossing Your Arms

The arms are crossed in front of the chest

Turn the palms of the hands outward

Close slowly forty-nine times. . .

Stand with your legs slightly apart and your feet firmly on the ground. The upper torso is straight, but not in an unnatural, bolt-upright position. The head should be in line with the body, and the eyes should face the front. The mouth is closed and the tongue lies on the upper palate in order to close off the circulation of energy of the two meridians.

. . .and again stretch the fingers

The shoulders should be relaxed and your arms should hang down loosely. Bend the knees in a slight squatting position, without straining yourself. When viewed from the top, the knees should not extend beyond the toes. The vertex "Bai Hui" should again be the fixing point from which your whole body seems to hang. Cross your arms in front of your chest, with the right palm facing left and the left palm facing right, both perpendicular to the lower arms. The elbows should hang as loosely and relaxed as possible. The right arm should be touching the body and the left arm should be in front of the right. The fingertips should be in front of your nipples. The entire body should be completely relaxed and your breathing calm and natural.

Now close the fingers of both hands at the same time, as if grasping for something. When you open them again, arch the fingers backwards tightly. Be sure that your shoulders are not pulled upwards involuntarily, and stay relaxed. Repeat this exercise 49 times.

Remain motionless and wait for the Qi in your fingertips to make itself noticeable. This will appear as a slight vibration that gradually increases in intensity on its way up the lower arms, elbows, and shoulders.

Now reverse the arms and repeat the exercise until you feel the Qi in your fingertips again.

Bend the knees as deep as possible

Crossing Your Arms

Most of the time you will not feel the vibration of Qi spontaneously. However, with patience and regular practice, the energy paths of the body—which most people are not even conscious of, or which may be affected by a wrong lifestyle--will be activated and restored.

In doing this exercise, the entire body will become healthier on the whole and can function better. The effect of Qi, which you have lured out from your body, gives you the feeling of a stream passing through your arms to your shoulders and your neck.

SUMMARY OF EXERCISE FIFTEEN

"CROSSING YOUR ARMS"

Stand with your legs slightly apart.

Your arms are crossed in front of your chest, bent at the elbows, with the left arm in front of the right. Your hands point upwards.

Tightly arch your hands backwards and then relax them again. Repeat this 49 times.

Wait for the Qi to vibrate from your fingertips to your arms and your shoulders.

Reverse the arms and repeat the exercise.

Crossing Your Arms

The Sixteenth Exercise

Presenting the Pearl

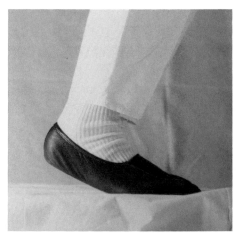

The heel is lifted slightly

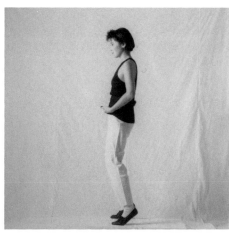

The legs are slightly bent

With the palms of the hands upward at the navel

From the usual starting position, take a step to the left, so that the legs are wide apart. Bend your knees to the extent that you can stay squatted in this position for a period of time without straining yourself. The knees should be directly over the instep of the feet, and not extended beyond the tips of the toes.

The upper torso should remain straight and upright, with the shoulders relaxed. The head should be upright and the eyes should face the front. The mouth should be closed with the tongue lying on the upper palate, thus shutting off the circulation of energy of the two main meridians.

Now place your hands with the palms facing upward, at the level of your navel. The fingertips should be about two finger-widths apart from each other. The elbows should be on each side of the body. Lift your heels from the ground.

Turn your head three times to the left, three times to the right, and then look to the front again. Now close and open your fingers nine times. As in the previous exercise, the fingers

Close the hands slowly nine times. . .

. . .and stretch them out completely again

When Qi flows correctly. . .

Presenting the Pearl

. . .move the hands up and down. . .

. . .between the chest and the abdomen

should be tightly arched backwards when you open them this way.

Wait in this position for the Qi to vibrate from the fingertips through the arms and shoulders to the entire body. When this vibration begins to take place, move your lower arms up and down slowly from the chest to the starting position, slightly below the navel. This movement only involves the arms and hands below the elbows. The rest of the body should be completely relaxed.

At first, a definite sign of flowing Qi, such as an involuntary vibration of the limbs, may not occur.

But when the body slowly begins to rediscover its forgotten energy paths, you should feel the Qi. It can take a while for this energy to start flowing strongly. Therefore, you should wait for the first signs of Qi, such as a numbness in the fingers, a slight prickling, or a feeling like an electric current flowing through your body.

When such sensations come, you can stimulate the further flow of Qi by

shaking the limbs involved until your body's own energy "takes over."

Exercise 16 is especially effective because it activates one of the main paths of the flow of energy, which lies on the front side of your body, leading from the abdomen to the head.

At the same time, it promotes "inner breathing," a circulation of energy that starts from the point "Yung Chuan" on the sole of your feet, and goes through the legs, back, arms, hands, and back of the shoulders into the upper torso, hips, and back to the legs.

This exercise is especially effective for kidney problems, problems of the inner organs, and general weaknesses. After just a short period of practice, you will notice improvement.

"PRESENTING THE PEARL"

Squat slightly with your legs apart.

Lift your heels off the ground.

With your palms facing upward, hold both hands at navel level.

Turn your head to the left three times and to the right three times, and then face the front.

Tightly arch your hands backward and then relax them nine times.

Without moving anymore, wait for the vibration of Qi to start in your fingertips and move into the arms and then into the shoulders.

Once you feel the Qi, move your hands up and down between the abdomen and the chest.

96

Presenting the Pearl

The Seventeenth Exercise

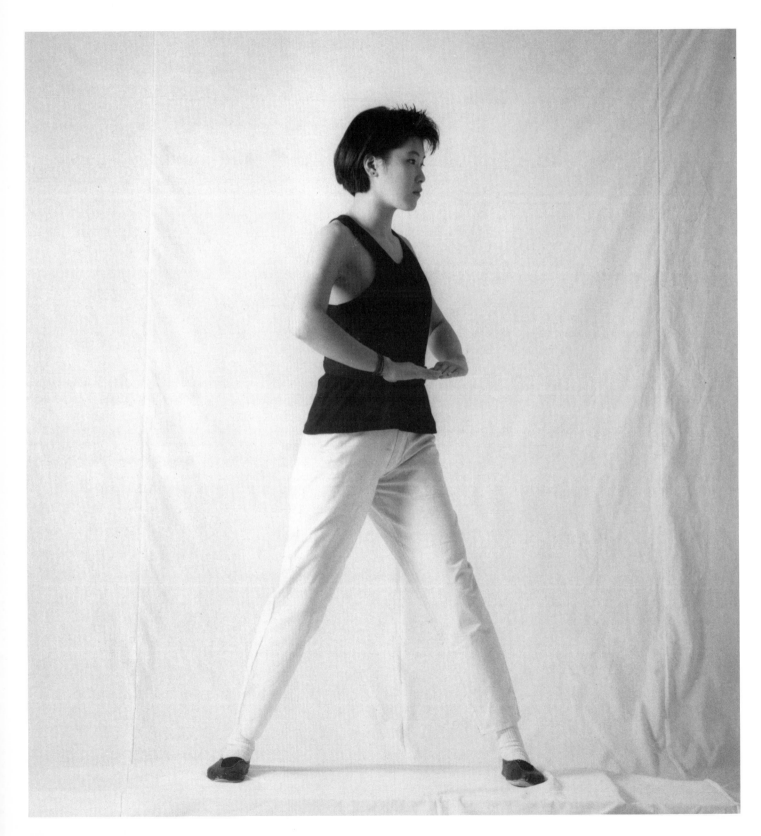

Turning Your Body

Stretch your legs far apart, palms down

The legs are firmly on the floor as the upper body turns first left

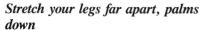

Begin Exercise Seventeen in the same position as you did the previous exercise, with your legs a little further apart and in a slight squat. The soles of the feet should be firmly on the floor. Your buttocks should be tightened and your back straight. Your neck and back of the head form a vertical line.

Face forward and look straight ahead. The mouth is closed and the teeth slightly clenched. The tongue lies on the upper palate, shutting off the circulation of energy between the two main meridians along the axis of symmetry of your body. Your hands should be placed in front of your chest as in the previous exercise, with palms down. Lower your hands to the height of your navel and leave four finger-widths of space between both hands. The wrists should be aligned with the stretched hands. The angle of your elbows does not change throughout the whole exercise.

In this position, bend and stretch your fingers nine times, making sure that they arch backwards tightly each time.

Now turn 90 degrees to the left and 90 degrees to the right with your upper torso. Repeat this movement at least nine times, but no more than 36

and then right

Stretch the hands thirty-six times. . .

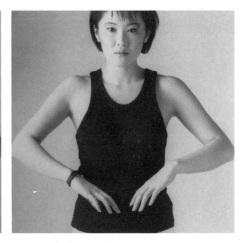

. . .and slowly close

Turning Your Body

times. While turning, the position of your hands in front of your body should not change. Your knees should always remain relaxed and face the front.

Now return to the starting position of Exercise Seventeen and wait for the Qi to spread from your fingertips to your arms and shoulders, and then through your neck to the entire body.

Again you can allow the vibration of Qi to last as long as you wish, or you can control the vibration by tensing your muscles.

Exercise Seventeen helps redistribute and equalize the energy which has gathered and settled in your body. Fields of energy that remain stagnant in various parts of the body can lead to sickness and pain.

Through this exercise, the stagnant energy will be led to the "belt meridian"—an energy path that is at the level of your waist—and, by turning your body, this energy will be redistributed evenly. You also use Exercise Seventeen to offset any unhealthy side effects of meditation, which gather an unnatural amount of energy in the upper part of the body.

SUMMARY OF EXERCISE SEVENTEEN

"TURNING YOUR BODY"

Squat slightly, with your legs apart.

Lower your hands to your navel, with palms facing down.

Arch your hands back and then relax them 9 to 36 times.

From your hips, turn your upper torso 9 to 36 times 90 degrees to the left and 90 degrees to the right.

Wait in the starting position for the vibration of Qi in your fingertips, which continues up your arms to your shoulders.

Turning Your Body

The Eighteenth Exercise

Strengthening Your Body

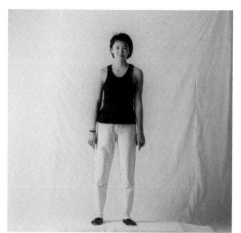

Spread your legs apart

Hands stretched forward

Palms of hands forward, bend knees as deeply and comfortably as possible

From the usual starting position, take a step to the left so that your legs are wide apart. Bend your knees so that you are in a slight squatting position, but only to the extent that you can stay in that position for an extended period of time without straining yourself. The knees should be exactly over the instep of the feet, and should not extend beyond tips of the toes. The buttocks are tightened, the chest should not protrude unnaturally, and the upper part of the back should be bent slightly forward. The lower part of the abdomen, below the navel, should be entirely relaxed, or "as soft as cotton," as the Chinese say.

Your mouth should be closed, teeth lightly clenched, and your tongue on the upper palate in order to close off the circulation of energy of the two meridians. Your whole body is fixed on the vertex "Bai Hui."

Now lift your arms horizontally in front of your body to shoulder height. The elbows are bent slightly, the palms face the front, and the fingers point upwards. but they should not be raised over the level of your shoulders.

In this position, close your hands and then stretch them so that they are flexed back tightly. The movement should only be in your hands. The rest of your body should be completely relaxed and stationary.

Repeat the bending and stretching of your fingers up to 49 times. Then, with your hands in the stretched position, wait for the vibration of Qi in your fingertips. It will pass through

Slowly close the hands forty-nine times. . .

the arms and shoulders to the entire body. Make sure that the whole body is fixed on the point "Bai Hui" when this vibration takes place.

If you allow the Qi to vibrate for a period of time and then curl up your toes, you will feel a tingling sensation at the lowest part of your soles, the point "Yung Chuan." It will feel like either a stream flowing there or just a warm sensation. This sensation can

. . .and stretch them out completely again

103

continue up your legs. Your arms may sense a numbness, as if they had fallen asleep.

This is a good sign because it shows that you are making progress in these exercises. When the vibrations of Qi ends, you may also have the feeling of Qi circling in your chest, thus making your chest feel light and free.

SUMMARY OF EXERCISE EIGHTEEN

"STRENGTHENING YOUR BODY"

Spread your legs apart in a slightly squatting position.

Stretch your arms outwards horizontally in front of your body.

Your palms should face the front, fingers pointing upwards.

Stretch and then relax your hands 49 times.

In this position, wait for the vibration of Qi to occur in your fingertips, arms, and shoulders.

Strengthening Your Body

The Nineteenth Exercise

Swinging the Foot

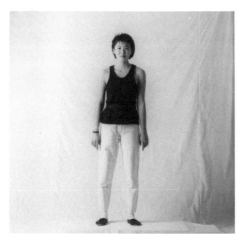

Slightly spread your legs apart, relax

In a continuous step, stretch the left toe nine times downward. . .

. . .then upwards. . .

Stand in the usual starting position, with legs slightly apart. The back should be straight and the head upright. The mouth is closed and the teeth are slightly clenched. The tongue lies on the upper palate and thus shuts off the circulation of energy of the two meridians along the axis of symmetry in the body. Concentrate on the "Bai Hui" vertex, which gives stability to your whole body and also serves as a pivot point

for the entire body. With the back of your hands facing frontwards, stretch your arms out to the sides, away from the body. The thumb and little finger should be stretched outwards, and the rest of the fingers should be bent with fingertips touching the palms. Now lift your left foot to an angle of 45 degrees—as if you were taking a small step to the front—and leave your leg hanging in the air. Point your toes downward, with the ankle

joint and knee joint loose and relaxed.

The right leg should be straight and firmly on the ground, and the shoulders should be relaxed and not tensed up.

Remain in this position for a while, until you sense the prickling feeling of Qi at the tip of your left foot. Then lift this foot until it is perpendicular to

and the leg completely stretched out behind

And everything repeated with the right foot

Swinging the Foot

Once again left, as seen from the side

the leg and again point it downward.

Repeat this exercise nine times. Then swing your leg at the same angle to the back of your body. Wait for the tingling feeling of Qi in the tip of your foot and let the vibration pass through your whole leg.

This vibration passes through the "Hui Yin" point that lies on the perineum (between the anus and the

genitals), then over the bladder and the abdomen, all the way to the navel, where it flows through the whole body with fresh energy.

Repeat this exercise with the other foot. The Nineteenth Exercise has its effect on all the organs of the pelvis minor—the bladder, the prostate, the kidney, and the colon.

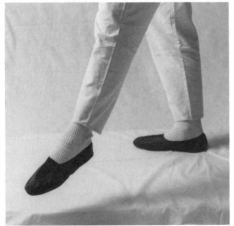

The toe is stretched out. . .

. . .and turned upward. . .

Swinging the Foot

. . .then stretched behind

The way the hand should be held during the whole exercise

SUMMARY OF EXERCISE NINETEEN

"SWINGING THE FOOT"

Stand with your legs slightly apart.

Stretch your arms sideways, with the fingers forming a fist.

Stretch out the thumb and little finger.

Lift your left foot to the front, with the toes pointing downwards.

Bend and stretch your left foot nine times.

With outstretched foot, move your left leg to the back of your body. Your foot should still remain in the air.

In this position, wait for the Qi that flows from your toes through your leg to the center of your body.

Repeat this exercise with the other leg.

Swinging the Foot

The Twentieth Exercise

Spread your legs apart, and with knees bent, lift arms to the side

Hold up the left leg, the foot remains relaxed. . .

. . .then the same with the right leg

From the usual starting position, take one large step to the left and squat slightly, facing the front. The buttocks are tightened, the upper torso is upright and relaxed, and the shoulders hang slightly downwards. The head should be straight, and the eyes should look to the front. Close the mouth, with teeth lightly clenched. The tongue lies on the upper palate in order to close off the circulation of energy of the two meridians. With open hands, lift the arms halfway up and away from each side of the body. Raise the index and middle fingers slightly, with the back of the hands facing frontwards.

It is very important to concentrate fully on your breathing in this exercise. So listen to it carefully.

Lift your left knee, letting your foot remain relaxed and hanging down. At the same time, tense up the muscles of your anus and then bring your leg slowly from the side to the front. Then loosen your anus muscles and let your foot down to the floor again. Do the same crane step with your right foot.

Take one crane step after another, moving forward, until you are standing on your left foot again after seven steps. Then turn the back of your hand around and start a crane gait with your right foot backwards. Take seven steps to the back until you are standing on your right foot again. Repeat this three times to the front and three times to the back, altogether taking 42 crane steps.

Concentrate on the power of Qi, which should be felt in the palms when going forward and in the back of your hands when going backwards.

After seven steps forward, put the right foot behind

And backwards seven steps

Walking Like a Crane

Walking Like a Crane

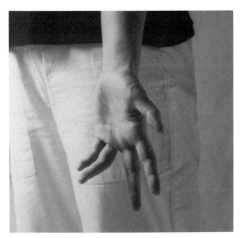

In going backwards, the palm of the hands face forward

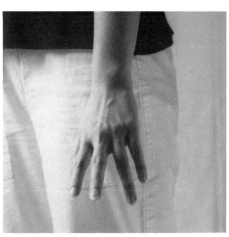

In going forwards, the palm of the hands face backwards

SUMMARY OF EXERCISE TWENTY

"WALKING LIKE A CRANE"

Squat with your legs wide apart.

Lift your arms at the sides of your body.

Lift your left knee and, with your foot hanging down, take a step with the left leg.

At the same time, tense up the muscles of your anus.

Repeat this step to the front with your right foot.

Take seven such steps to the front. During this movement, the back of your hand should be facing front.

Now take seven such steps backwards, beginning with the right foot. The back of your hands should be facing the back.

Altogether take 42 steps.

Walking Like a Crane